Reclaiming Our Narrative: A Citizen's Toolkit for Countering Identity-Based Disinformation

© 2025 Organization for Identity and Cultural Development (OICD)

Published by EMIC Press
OICD EMIC Limited, Oxford, UK

First Edition: 2025

ISBN: 978-0-9567316-1-6 (Paperback)
ISBN: 978-0-9567316-2-3 (eBook)

While the author and publisher have made every effort to ensure the accuracy and completeness of information contained in this book, we assume no responsibility for errors, inaccuracies, omissions, or any inconsistency herein. Any slights of people or organizations are unintentional.

This toolkit is provided as a resource for countering identity-based disinformation. It is intended for informational and educational purposes only and should not be considered a substitute for professional advice or training. Users are solely responsible for ensuring the ethical and appropriate use of this toolkit and the content it generates.

The OICD provides this guide as part of its not-for-profit mission. You can help sustain this vital work by sharing the open access PDF version (oicd.net/resources) or by purchasing print/e-book copies. All proceeds support the OICD's mission.

Acknowledgements: Primary Author: Dr. Bruce White; The OICD Advisory Board members provided critical feedback. Contributions from OICD key area advisors: Dr. Anna Kruglova, Dr. Susan Rottmann

www.oicd.net

Reclaiming Our Narratives

A Practical Guide to Countering Identity-Based Disinformation

Organization for Identity & Cultural Development

2025 1st Edition

Contents

1 What's Inside: A Practical Guide to Countering Identity-Based Disinformation

The Challenge: Identity-Based Disinformation (IBD)

Online and offline, a dangerous type of manipulation targets who we are at our core – our values, beliefs, and sense of belonging. Identity-Based Disinformation (IBD) isn't just disinformation by "fake news"; it's designed to play on our basic human needs (like the need to belong and feel safe) by offering narrow, divisive definitions of who we are. It creates false "us vs. them" choices, stirs up emotions like fear and anger, and thrives in echo chambers. The damage is real: it can break apart families, divide communities, weaken trust, and lead to violence.

Our Strategy: Positive Identity Expansion

Confronting the effects of this type of disinformation head-on may not be the most effective approach. When senses of identity are involved, confrontation can lead to defensiveness and further entrenchment. This guide offers a different approach: **Positive Identity Expansion**. Instead of directly attacking the disinformation, we focus on providing the targets of the disinformation (the people being manipulated) with the options they need to escape its influence and become stronger and more resilient.

We do this by creating and deploying **"Alternative Narratives"** – positive, real messages that:

1. **Meet Deep Needs:** Fulfill the same deep needs as the disinformation exploits (belonging, esteem, security) in healthy, inclusive ways.

2. **Broaden Identity:** Remind people how rich their lives, cultures, communities and identities really are, showing that seemingly conflicting values (e.g., traditional and modern, patriotic and critical) can coexist.

3. **Celebrate Diversity:** Showcase the positive diversity within the target audience's own culture in a way that resonates with them.

4. **Focus on the Positive:** Build up shared values and connections, staying positive.

Building Community Resilience

This approach helps individuals resist divisive messages, strengthening what we might call the "cultural immune system". By nurturing culturally accurate, complex and inclusive identities, communities naturally become more resistant to manipulation tactics that rely on oversimplification and division. The result is stronger social bonds and increased collective resilience against future disinformation campaigns which exploit identities.

The 7 Implementation Steps: A Quick Overview

This guide provides a practical, step-by-step process:

1. **Analyze the Disinformation Campaign:** Understand the specific messages, themes, emotions, needs exploited, and power dynamics at play.
2. **Define & Understand the Target Audience:** Deeply analyze the demographics, identities, values, needs, and information sources of the group being influenced by the identity-based disinformation.
3. **Develop Alternative Narratives:** Brainstorm positive values and strategies to fulfill needs inclusively, drawing on authentic cultural references.
4. **Identify Trusted Voices & Channels:** Determine who the audience trusts and where they get their information.
5. **Craft Your Messages:** Create specific, culturally resonant content (stories, images, videos) tailored for different platforms.
6. **Strategic Narrative Design:** Ensure messages provide authentic cultural celebration, not obvious counter-messaging, to optimize their effectiveness.
7. **Review, Refine & Share Responsibly:** Ethically review content, gather feedback, and share through trusted channels, monitoring impact.

Supporting Resources:

To further aid understanding and implementation, this guide includes worksheets, AI prompt examples, a glossary, academic references, and a section detailing relevant organizations and resources from the international counter-disinformation landscape.

Our Promise: Do No Harm

It is important to treat any work which interfaces with human identity seriously - it comes with a responsibility. The core principle is

Do No Harm. Our goal is to build bridges, encourage clear thinking, respect differences, be accurate, and focus on positive messaging and actions. We never attack individuals or groups for ANY reason (even those who develop and distribute identity-based disinformation campaigns - who we refer to as 'IBD agents' in this guide).

Who Is This For?

This guide is for concerned individuals of all types, people of all professions and none. Members of communities, parents, educators, leaders – anyone looking for practical ways to help their communities resist divisive messages. You don't need to be an expert. Your actions can make a real difference.

"...'ordinary ordinary' is where the real drama is. To win an information war you need to understand how propaganda exploits this ordinariness—and then outplay it."

— Pomerantsev, P. (2025). How to Win an Information War: The Propagandist Who Outwitted Hitler. London: Faber & Faber

2 The Power of Individual Action: A Call to Arms Against Identity-Based Disinformation

In our highly interconnected world, we all face a hidden but powerful threat: the spread and influence of identity-based disinformation (IBD). This form of disinformation is much more sophisticated and dangerous than just "fake news". Identity-based disinformation attacks us at the heart of who we are, targeting our values and sense of belonging. It is designed to deliberately harm and divide us. The damage can spread through all our relationships, dividing families, friends, communities, and whole societies. We see it through family gatherings gone silent, community bonds fraying and fracturing, and democratic institutions weakening.

The power of identity-based disinformation to erode our lives can seem overwhelming at a time of increasing polarization in our world. But there is hope, and it lies with you.

The Power of Individual Action

History has repeatedly demonstrated that successful resistance against persecution, division and marginalization is powered by individual courage and action. The Civil Rights Movement wasn't just Martin Luther King Jr.—it was Rosa Parks refusing to give up her seat, and countless everyday people joining boycotts, sit-ins, and marches. The women's suffrage movement succeeded because of the combined efforts of well known women like Emmeline Pankhurst and Susan B. Anthony, but there are thousands whose names we'll never know, who distributed pamphlets, organized meetings, and stood firm in their convictions.

These movements, and many others, demonstrate how individual actions, when multiplied across many courageous and motivated actors, create an unstoppable momentum to combat forces that seek to diminish the human spirit.

In today's world, this power of individual action is amplified, for better and worse, by modern technology. Smartphones deliver information (and disinformation) instantly, while social media algorithms often create personalized "echo chambers" where individuals primarily see content that confirms and plays to their existing views. This environment makes it simple for misinformation (unintentionally false information) and disinformation (intentionally false information) to spread rapidly and take root, as false messages are constantly reinforced. Individuals influenced by online falsehoods will likely end up spreading these on- and offline in a multitude of conversations in families, communities, workplaces and random encounters. A process aided by the fact that identity-based disinformation is designed to stir emotions and mobilize people to evangelize the very disinformation they have been exposed to. If we ever needed evidence to demonstrate that individuals can make a difference, look at the current state of the spread of disinformation and the resulting social and political polarization in our societies. This is caused by millions of individuals acting independently.

If there is an optimism to be had in any of this, it is that it all works in reverse. Positive, alternative messages which celebrate human capacities and cultures are also able to cascade through these same online networks, undoing and preventing further deliberate manipulation. While disinformation campaigns are often systematic and financially incentivised and resourced by bad actors who have an interest in dividing and harming us, by understanding their techniques and developing tools to respond and resist them, we can become part of an alternative independent network of courageous individual actors who seek to outcompete the harmful exploitation of our information environment.

By understanding the nature of identity-based disinformation and how it exploits this environment, our individual and collective contributions can potentially be more impactful than ever before. This guide has been developed to provide all of the key tools necessary for any individual to start their journey towards being part of this counterforce.

Alternative Narratives

Rather than directly confronting divisive identity-based disinformation messages, this guide will present a step-by-step approach to developing and deploying Alternative Narratives. Alternative narratives are collections of messages which celebrate the richness and diversity of a community's identity. Importantly, these messages are calibrated to fulfill the same psychological needs that their disinformation message counterparts exploit—belonging, self-esteem, security, significance etc.. Alternative narrative messages meet these needs in healthy, inclusive ways that expand rather than narrow the target audiences' sense of who they are.

In thinking about how transformative having alternative narratives in circulation might be, we might imagine an information environment in which every community experiencing identity-based disinformation messaging would also be exposed to many stories that celebrated diverse expressions of patriotism, religious practice, or cultural heritage. We might imagine social media feeds filled with examples of people who successfully navigate seemingly contradictory values—being both traditional and innovative, religious and scientific, patriotic and critical. We might imagine the cumulative effect of thousands of such messages, creating a cultural environment more resistant to divisive manipulation.

This is not the information environment we live in now. But this reality awaits us if we have the courage to stand up, individually and collectively, to intelligently challenge the destructive force of identity-based disinformation in all of our societies.

What This Toolkit Does (and Doesn't Do)

This toolkit provides a step-by-step method to create messages that counter Identity-Based Disinformation (IBD). Specifically, it presents the techniques you need to:

- **Analyze IBD Narratives**: Understand the messages being spread and the underlying needs they exploit.

- **Identify Positive Values**: Find the positive values and identity expressions that can be amplified to counter the IBD.

- **Develop and Deploy Alternative Narratives**: Create messages that celebrate these positive values and expand the target audience's sense of self.

- **Find Cultural References**: Discover relevant examples from history, literature, and popular culture that support your message and make the delivery of alternative narratives effective.

- **Leverage AI Tools**: Provides guidance and prompts to use AI assistants for analysis and narrative creation, helping to streamline the process (and offering potential to scale up impact).

- **Access Supporting Materials**: Provides worksheets, a glossary, academic references, and a chapter on relevant organizations and resources to deepen understanding and aid implementation.

- **Join the Community**: Offers ways for you to contribute your experiences, suggest improvements, and collaborate on improving this guide.

This guide's unique contribution lies in its focus on ***positive identity expansion*** as a primary strategy, equipping individuals *without* specialized technical skills to create resonant, *alternative narratives* that build psychological resilience within communities affected by identity-based disinformation. This practical approach is derived from a more expansive EMIC methodology developed by the Organization for Identity and Cultural Development (OICD), which offers systematic and scalable solutions to IBD prevention and response (see chapter on Organizations and Resources for Countering IBD).

What this toolkit doesn't do:

- **Help to Debunk False Claims**: This guide doesn't contain any fact-checking or debunking tools. Our focus is on building resilience at a deeper level, addressing the psychological and cultural needs that IBD exploits.

- **Target or Attack the IBD Agent or Their Message**: This toolkit is strictly about promoting positive values within the target audience. We never create content that attacks, demonizes, or stereotypes any other group, including those responsible for the IBD messaging.

- **Replace Good Human Judgment**: This toolkit provides a framework, but your knowledge of the target audience and the specific situation is essential. You must carefully review, adapt, and refine any messages you create.

- **Guarantee Success**: No single set of tools can guarantee success against disinformation. This is one piece of a larger puzzle, and the approach within should be considered for use alongside other established efforts like media literacy education and community building (again see the chapter Organizations and Resources for Countering IBD).

A Practical Strategy

This toolkit contains a practical strategy based on solid evidence about how identity works and how psychological and social transformation happens. When we provide multiple pathways for people to express their values and meet their fundamental needs, we strengthen their resilience against narratives that offer only narrow, divisive options.

The power of this approach is that it doesn't require significant resources or specialized expertise. Anyone can participate—parents concerned about their children's online environment, community leaders hoping to heal local divisions, educators wanting to foster critical thinking, or simply individuals troubled by the growing polarization in our society. This guide is designed for all such concerned individuals, community members, faith leaders, and anyone seeking practical ways to foster resilience against divisive narratives in their networks – no specialist background required.

Of course, if you do bring relevant skill sets to this effort, you may find it particularly straightforward and effective. If you work as part of an organization tasked with engaging individuals and communities in some way, the OICD and other related organizations may be able to offer additional support and tools (Again, see the chapter on Organizations and Resources for Countering IBD).

The Power of Collective Action

Every post you share, every conversation you guide, every story you tell that expands rather than restricts identity options is a meaningful contribution. As we have emphasized in the previous section, while individually these actions might seem small, together, they can compound to build a 'cultural immune system' against the destructive force of identity-based disinformation.

By taking up this toolkit and putting its strategies into practice, you're joining an important movement to protect our communities, support democracy, and make society stronger. Where able, we encourage you to connect with others and contribute to the ongoing development of this resource – learn how in the Chapter Join the Community.

The Road Ahead

Those who spread division can be well-funded and sophisticated in their tactics. But they cannot match the authenticity, creativity, and deep community connections that you bring to this work.

Your voice matters. Your actions count. And together with others taking similar steps in communities across the world, you can help build a society more resistant to manipulation and more capable of emerging from division into unity and cohesion.

The toolkit awaits. The time to act is now.

3 Understanding Identity-Based Disinformation

Identity-based disinformation (IBD) represents a particularly harmful threat to our social fabric. Unlike conventional disinformation that simply spreads incorrect facts, IBD specifically targets and manipulates how people understand themselves and their place in the world.

At its core, IBD 'weaponizes' identity—the fundamental sense of who we are, including our values, beliefs, sense of cultural heritage, and group affiliations. This weaponization seeks to fray human bonds, divide communities and cause harm to our societies. It operates by exploiting our deepest human needs for belonging, self-esteem, significance, and security, offering narrow and rigid definitions of identity as the only path to fulfilling these needs.

This toolkit primarily addresses identity-based *disinformation* – the deliberate weaponization of identity. While unintentional *misinformation* can also be damaging, the strategies here are tailored to counter the specific manipulative intent behind IBD.

Key Characteristics of IBD

When you encounter IBD, you might notice several telltale characteristics:

1. **False Choices**: It creates false choices, suggesting you must choose between aspects of your identity that can actually coexist—for example, that you can't be both religious and scientific, traditional and progressive, or patriotic and critical of your country's policies.

2. **Emotional Manipulation**: It employs emotionally charged language and imagery designed to trigger fear, anger, or resentment. These strong emotions can override critical thinking, making it easier to accept divisive narratives.

3. **Echo Chambers**: IBD thrives in echo chambers where people are primarily exposed to information that confirms existing beliefs, gradually narrowing one's identity options and worldview.

4. **Othering**: It often involves the demonization of an "other" individual and/or group, portrayed as threatening or inferior. This fuels division and creates cycles of increasing polarization which become increasingly difficult to redress.

5. **Use of Reasoning Fallacies**: While not unique to IBD, these campaigns often employ flawed logic, such as appeals to questionable authority or common opinion, red herrings, begging the question, slippery slope arguments, and other fallacies common in propaganda.

The Impact of IBD

The consequences of IBD extend far beyond online and offline arguments:

- Friendships dissolve as identity conflicts make mutual understanding increasingly difficult

- Families find themselves unable to communicate across political divides

- Community organizations struggle with internal conflicts

- Democratic institutions weaken as citizens lose trust in shared facts and values

- In extreme cases, IBD can contribute to radicalization and even violence

What makes IBD particularly challenging is that directly confronting or debunking it often backfires. When someone's sense of self is deeply tied to a particular belief or group identity, challenging that belief feels like a personal attack, leading to defensiveness and deeper entrenchment.

We will become more familiar with the core approach of this guide - **Positive Identity Expansion** - in the next chapter: an approach which offers an alternative to direct confrontation. For now, we can understand that Positive Identity Expansion seeks to provide multiple ways for people to express their values and meet their fundamental needs, helping build resilience against IBD narratives that offer only narrow, divisive options.

Factors Contributing to Identity-Based Vulnerability

While IBD targets our sense of self, certain experiences can make us particularly susceptible to these IBD narratives. Traumas, societal transformations, and economic insecurity don't operate separately from identity—they directly shape how secure we feel in who we are and our place in the world.

Studies show that individuals who have undergone significant societal changes or experienced personal trauma often develop deep-seated feelings of uncertainty about their place in the world (see Chapter on Academic Research Supporting the Toolkit). When these experiences coincide with economic hardship or perceived scarcity, people become particularly susceptible to narratives that offer simple explanations and clear enemies. The combination of material insecurity and threats to one's sense of self-worth creates ideal conditions for divisive ideologies that promote rigid us-versus-them thinking.

How Identity-Based Disinformation Works: Understanding the Tactics

Research has demonstrated that identity-based disinformation (IBD) is particularly effective because it targets core aspects of identity—values, beliefs, and group affiliations—to exploit fundamental human needs that all humans share.

To effectively counter IBD, we need to understand how it works. It's crucial to analyze not just the IBD agent's manipulative intent, but, even more importantly, *why the narrative resonates with the receiver* – what genuine need does it fulfill for them?

Core Human Needs Targeted by IBD

IBD tactics work by exploiting fundamental human needs which include:

1. **Belonging and Connection**

    - The need to feel accepted and valued by others

    - Includes family bonds, friendships, community ties, ethnic, religious, political, regional and national senses of belonging

2. **Self-Worth and Significance**

    - The need to feel valued, respected, and significant

    - Includes desire for recognition and feeling that your life has purpose

3. **Equality and Justice**

    - The need to be treated fairly and see balance in personal life and society

    - Includes concerns about rights, justice and equitable treatment

4. **Security and Safety**

- The need to feel protected from threats

- Includes physical safety, psychological security and stability

IBD Manipulation Tactics

1. Promising a Narrow Identity

IBD often offers a seemingly easy way to meet these needs, but at a cost. It says, "You can belong, feel significant, and be safe, but only if you define yourself in this very specific, narrow way." It might emphasize one aspect of our identity (like nationality, religion, or political views) while demanding that we reject or downplay other parts of ourselves. This narrowing almost always results in an "us vs. them" mentality which supports states of polarization and conflict.

2. Exploiting Emotions

IBD uses emotionally charged language and images – things that make us feel angry, afraid, resentful, or insecure. These strong emotions often trigger our human needs thus making it more likely to believe false information which exploits those needs.

3. Creating Echo Chambers

IBD thrives in places where people mostly hear information that confirms their existing beliefs. This reinforces biases and makes it harder to see other perspectives. Think of it like being trapped in a room where everyone agrees with you – you might start to believe that everyone in the world thinks the same way.

4. Attacking the "Other"

IBD often demonizes another group, making them seem dangerous or threatening. This fuels the kinds of division and harm that is often the purpose of the IBD: creating 'enemies' from people that might have been friends or neighbours, and further helping to exploit needs such as security, status and belonging.

Power Dynamics in IBD

Understanding the tactics of IBD must include an understanding of how **power** shapes the landscape of disinformation. Societal power imbalances – based on factors like class, wealth, political influence, ethnicity, gender, social status – significantly affect how IBD is created, spread, and received. Crucially, these power dynamics often intersect with the exploitation of core human needs discussed earlier.

These aspects of power are often in play alongside IBD messaging campaigns:

1. **Shaping Dominant Narratives:** Groups with power may control or heavily influence certain media platforms and political discourses. This allows them to establish certain narratives as "normal" or "common sense," often elevating the perceived **self-esteem, status, and significance** of those who align with the dominant view while marginalizing others

and portraying alternative perspectives as less credible or fringe.

2. **Access to Resources:** Creating and disseminating sophisticated disinformation campaigns at scale usually requires resources – funding, technical expertise, media access, and networks (most of the case studies we consider in the next chapter include resourcing from a domestic or foreign state). Groups with greater power often have disproportionately more resources, enabling them to amplify their messages far more effectively. This allows them to scale their promises of fulfillment of needs like **security or belonging**, sometimes offering enhanced **self-esteem or significance** to those who adopt their narrow identity narrative, while drowning out counter-narratives from less powerful groups.

3. **Ability to Implement Change (or Resist It):** Power influences who gets heard in policy debates and whose concerns are addressed. IBD can be used by powerful actors to maintain the status quo or resist changes that might challenge their position (and thus their perceived **significance or status**), often by targeting groups advocating for change. Conversely, less powerful groups may struggle to make their alternative/counter-narratives heard or to implement positive changes due to resource limitations and lack of access to influential channels, impacting their own sense of **agency and significance**.

4. **Unequal Starting Points for Narratives:** An existing dominant narrative, often backed by societal power structures,

carries inherent weight and can shape baseline perceptions of **status and legitimacy**. Alternative narratives from less powerful groups must often work harder to gain traction and overcome ingrained biases or skepticism fueled by the power imbalance.

5. **The Power of Reversing Power:** Power dynamics in IBD are not solely top-down. As the case studies in the next chapter illustrate, power can be exploited in multiple directions. Less powerful actors can use IBD to attack institutions or perceived elites, aiming to erode trust and gain influence by appealing to grievances (tapping into needs for **justice or significance** among their audience). Conversely, powerful entities (governments, political campaigns, dominant social groups) can weaponize disinformation to demonize others, create a perception of threat, maintain control, and justify policies that harm marginalized communities, frequently promising enhanced **status, security, or significance** to their followers in the process.

Understanding the role of power adds a critical layer to our understanding of how IBD works. The case studies in the following chapter vividly illustrate how these power imbalances are exploited in practice, often manipulating fundamental human needs by creating 'us vs. them' scenarios where one group's status is elevated by diminishing another's.

Again, understanding IBD is the first step toward countering its effects. With this knowledge, we can begin to recognize how IBD exploits human psychology and set out to apply the Positive Identity Expansion strategies in this toolkit to support a comprehensive approach to countering and building resilience against its influence.

4 Historical and Contemporary Examples of IBD

Understanding how IBD works becomes clearer when we examine real-world cases, both historical and contemporary. The following examples demonstrate how identity has been weaponized across different contexts, cultures, and time periods through IBD campaigns. Each case illustrates the serious consequences of identity weaponization, while also offering valuable lessons for recognition and prevention.

Example 1: Nazi Anti-Jewish Propaganda (1930s–40s, Germany)

- **Target Audience:** German people.

- **"Other":** Jewish people in Germany and occupied Europe.

- **Nature of Disinformation:** The Nazi regime disseminated virulent anti-Semitic lies and stereotypes – e.g. that Jews were "subhuman" and to blame for Germany's ills. Nazi publications like *Der Stürmer* ran grotesque caricatures and false accusations (such as world conspiracy and ritual crimes) to demonize Jews. This hate propaganda dehumanized Jewish people and portrayed them as an existential threat.

- **IBD Tactics & Identity Narrowing:** This campaign exemplifies **extreme Othering**, portraying Jews as fundamentally alien and malevolent. It used **Emotional Manipulation** (fear, disgust, resentment) through shocking imagery and fabricated stories. By blaming Jews for national problems, it **Promised a Narrow Identity** to Germans: a path to restored **Self-Esteem**, **Significance**, and **Security** was offered *only* through embracing an "Aryan," anti-Semitic identity and rejecting any shared humanity with Jews. This created a **False Choice** between being a "loyal German" and showing empathy towards Jews, effectively **narrowing German identity** to exclude compassion and critical thought regarding the regime's 'other'. The need for **Belonging** within the "Volksgemeinschaft" (community of The People) was made conditional on accepting this hateful ideology.

- **Spread:** Through state-controlled media (newspapers, posters, radio broadcasts, films) under Joseph Goebbels' Ministry of Propaganda. Nazi propagandists saturated public discourse with these falsehoods, using the latest technology of the time to reach millions. Schools and rallies also echoed the disinformation, creating pervasive **Echo Chambers**.

- **Actors Involved:** The Nazi government and Nazi Party officials were the primary drivers. Key figures included Propaganda Minister Goebbels and publisher Julius Streicher (editor of *Der Stürmer*). Streicher and others used their platforms to incite hatred; Streicher was later convicted of inciting genocide.

- **Real-World Consequences:** The disinformation succeeded in fostering broad societal acceptance of anti-Jewish policies, from legal discrimination (Nuremberg Laws) to violence (Kristallnacht). It **played an integral role in the ultimate genocide**, creating public indifference or support for the Holocaust. By dehumanizing Jews and narrowing the acceptable scope of German identity, Nazi propaganda paved the way for the murder of 6 million Jewish people.

- **Debunking/Response:** At the time, independent voices within Germany were silenced. Allies countered Nazi propaganda with their own information campaigns during WWII, but the Nazi lies were fully discredited only after the war – through the exposure of Nazi atrocities and trials like Nuremberg. Today, Holocaust education and remembrance serve to debunk Nazi disinformation, and many countries ban Nazi hate symbols and Holocaust denial. Scholarly research (e.g., by the US Holocaust Memorial Museum) documents how Nazi hate speech led directly to genocide.

Example 2: Rwandan Genocide Hate Radio (1994, Rwanda)

- **Target Audience:** Hutu population.

- **"Other":** Tutsi ethnic minority (and moderate Hutus).

- **Nature of Disinformation:** Extreme hate speech and false claims were spread to justify exterminating Tutsis. The notorious Radio Télévision Libre des Mille Collines (RTLM) repeatedly referred to Tutsis as inyenzi or "cockroaches" and accused them of plotting to enslave Hutus. It broadcast *disinformation* that Tutsis had perpetrated attacks or were betraying Rwanda, stoking fear and hatred. When the genocide began, RTLM read out names and locations of Tutsis, falsely labeling them enemies, effectively issuing killing directives. Hate-filled print media (e.g. *Kangura* magazine) also published fabricated "plans" of Tutsi domination (like the bogus "Hutu Ten Commandments"), adding to the disinformation.

- **IBD Tactics & Identity Narrowing:** This was a brutal campaign of **Othering** (dehumanization as "cockroaches") coupled with intense **Emotional Manipulation** (stoking existential fear and hatred). It **Promised a Narrow Identity** where Hutu **Security** and **Significance** were achievable *only* through ethnic solidarity against Tutsis. It created a deadly **False Choice**: kill or be killed/enslaved, thus **narrowing Hutu identity** to exclude any possibility of coexistence or shared Rwandan nationality. **Belonging** within the Hutu community became contingent on participating in or supporting the violence against the Tutsi "enemy."

- **Spread:** Primarily through **radio**, which had a wide audience in Rwanda. RTLM broadcasters interwove propaganda with popular music to attract listeners – literally providing "music to kill to," as survivors recall. The disinformation also spread via word-of-mouth and print leaflets. The radio's messages reached towns and villages across the country in real-time, urging listeners to hunt down their neighbors, functioning as a powerful **Echo Chamber**.

- **Actors Involved:** Hutu extremist leaders and the interim Rwandan government were behind the broadcasts. RTLM was co-founded and funded by figures like Félicien Kabuga (a businessman) and operated by Hutu hardliners. Announcers like Kantano Habimana and Valérie Bemeriki became the on-air voices of hate. The government and militia (Interahamwe) coordinated with RTLM – effectively using it as a genocidal command-and-control channel.

- **Real-World Consequences:** The impact was catastrophic. The incendiary disinformation from RTLM **"helped spur and direct killings"**, actively fomenting the 1994 genocide in which 800,000 Tutsis (and sympathetic Hutus) were slaughtered. Perpetrators often carried a machete in one hand and a radio in the other. The broadcasts intensified the violence and guided mobs to victims; areas that initially hesitated to participate were convinced by the relentless false radio narratives. This makes Rwanda a textbook case of media-fueled genocide, driven by the successful narrowing of identity along ethnic lines.

- **Debunking/Response:** In the aftermath, the international community recognized the role of disinformation in the genocide. The International Criminal Tribunal for Rwanda prosecuted RTLM's executives: founders Ferdinand Nahimana and Jean Bosco Barayagwiza were convicted of incitement to genocide and sentenced to life in prison. This set a precedent that media propaganda can be a crime against humanity. Post-genocide Rwandan governments banned ethnically-based hate speech; today, memorials and education in Rwanda explicitly highlight how radio lies led to real-world atrocity. The case is often cited by the UN as evidence that *"hate speech coupled with disinformation can lead to... large-scale violence"* (Say No To Hate | United Nations in Montenegro).

Example 3: Anti-Rohingya "Fake News" in Myanmar (2010s, Myanmar)

- **Target Audience:** Buddhist majority in Myanmar.

- **"Other":** The Rohingya Muslim minority in Myanmar (also referred to pejoratively as "Bengalis" by opponents).

- **Nature of Disinformation:** A flood of false stories and hateful rhetoric portrayed Rohingya as dangerous outsiders. Myanmar's military and ultra-nationalists pushed narratives that **Rohingya were illegal immigrants, terrorists, or were even "burning their own villages"** to tarnish the government. Graphic fake images spread – for example, pictures from unrelated conflicts (showing mutilated bodies) were posted with captions falsely blaming Rohingya for atrocities. Propaganda also denied atrocities against Rohingya, claiming reports of ethnic cleansing were fabricated.

The cumulative message of this disinformation painted the Rohingya as a dire threat to Buddhists, fueling hatred and fear.

- **IBD Tactics & Identity Narrowing:** This campaign relied heavily on **Othering** (labeling Rohingya as foreign, dangerous, deceitful) and **Emotional Manipulation** (using fake images and stories to incite fear, anger, and disgust). It **Promised a Narrow Identity** for the Buddhist majority, suggesting that national **Security** and cultural continuity could only be maintained by embracing a nationalist identity that excluded and distrusted Rohingya. This effectively **narrowed Myanmar identity** by making Buddhist nationalism seem essential and incompatible with tolerance for the Rohingya minority. The need for **Belonging** was reinforced by positioning the majority against a common "enemy."

- **Spread:** Largely via **social media – especially Facebook**, which was/is ubiquitous in Myanmar. The false claims and inflammatory posts spread on Facebook pages and groups, often by accounts tied to the Myanmar military's psychological operations. Content also spread through Facebook Messenger, WhatsApp, and local-language media. Hardline Buddhist monks (like Ashin Wirathu) echoed disinformation in sermons and YouTube videos. Because for many in Myanmar "Facebook *is* the internet," these falsehoods circulated unchecked to millions, often generating thousands of shares and comments, creating potent **Echo Chambers**. State media and officials at times amplified the same narratives.

- **Actors Involved:** Key actors were Myanmar's military (Tatmadaw) and nationalist influencers. A military-led online campaign (using troll accounts) coordinated much of the anti-Rohingya fake news. Ultranationalist Buddhist groups (e.g. Ma Ba Tha) and certain monks became prominent spreaders of the conspiracies. Some civilian extremists and expatriate propagandists joined in on social platforms. Facebook eventually identified and banned dozens of accounts linked to Myanmar military officials for this coordinated disinformation campaign.

- **Real-World Consequences:** The disinformation directly stoked violence and justified the military's brutal operations. Hate speech and false accusations on Facebook have been **"stoking violence against the Rohingya"**, contributing to public support (or indifference) for a 2017 crackdown that the UN later deemed a possible genocide. On the ground, this meant mass killings, village burnings, and the exodus of over 700,000 Rohingya to Bangladesh. Mobs, inflamed by rumors (for instance, a fake rape or murder attributed to Rohingya), engaged in lynchings and arson. A UN investigator concluded that Facebook had become a tool for ethnic cleansing in Myanmar (Why Facebook is losing the war on hate speech in Myanmar - Reuters). The social fabric between Buddhist and Muslim communities was severely damaged as identities were narrowed and polarized, and the Rohingya remain largely displaced and disenfranchised.

- **Debunking/Response:** Belatedly, some responses emerged. International media and human rights groups exposed many of the false claims (e.g., BBC and *The New York Times* debunked fake photos and atrocity denials). In 2018, Facebook admitted it **"was too slow to prevent the spread of hate and misinformation"** in Myanmar and took action – it banned the accounts of top generals and hate groups, and improved content moderation for Myanmar language. Local Myanmar fact-checkers and civil society have since tried to monitor propaganda. However, much damage was already done; trust was eroded. The UN continues to call for account-ability, and organizations like Amnesty have documented Facebook's role, pushing for stronger oversight to prevent such disinformation-driven violence in the future.

Example 4: "Trojan Horse" Hoax in UK Schools (2014, United Kingdom)

- **Target Audience:** Wider British public.

- **"Other":** British Muslims, specifically Muslim educators and students in Birmingham.

- **Nature of Disinformation:** A fraudulent letter dubbed the "Trojan Horse" outlined an alleged Islamist plot to infiltrate public schools and impose strict Islamic practices. The letter – supposedly written by an extremist to a co-conspirator – detailed a five-step conspiracy to take over school gover-nance, force out non-Muslim staff, segregate genders, and radicalize curricula. Nonetheless, its sensational claims were reported as fact, creating a narrative that Muslim teachers and governors across Birmingham were orchestrating a secret extremist takeover. This unleashed a moral panic about "Islamization" of schools.

- **IBD Tactics & Identity Narrowing:** This hoax employed **Othering** by portraying civically engaged Muslims as a hidden threat. It relied heavily on **Emotional Manipulation**, stoking fear and suspicion (Islamophobia) about the safety of children and "British values." It implicitly **Promised a Narrow Identity** where **Security** and cultural continuity were linked to vigilance against Muslim influence in public institutions. This **narrowed the identity** of both British Muslims (casting suspicion on their participation in civic life) and the broader public (promoting distrust over inclusion). It presented a **False Choice** between supporting Muslim community involvement in schools and protecting national values/children.

- **Spread:** The disinformation spread first via **leaks to media**. The anonymous letter was sent to the Birmingham City Council in late 2013, and by early 2014 it was leaked to national press. Tabloid and mainstream newspapers ran alarming headlines (e.g., "Islamist plot dubbed 'Trojan Horse' to replace teachers with radicals"), largely accepting the letter's claims. Social media further amplified the hysteria, and discussions on talk radio and TV framed it as a major security issue. Authorities reacted publicly: the Department for Education and Ofsted (schools inspectorate) launched investigations, which kept the story in headlines for months. In effect, unverified claims in a hoax document gained widespread credibility through media and officialdom, creating an **Echo Chamber**.

- **Actors Involved:** Unknown individuals authored the hoax letter (motive still unclear, possibly a personal feud or to discredit certain educators). Nationalist and Islamophobic voices then seized upon it – some media outlets showed little skepticism, and politicians like then-Education Secretary aggressively responded as if the plot were real. Ofsted inspectors and others entered schools looking for evidence of the "plot." The saga was fueled by an existing climate of distrust toward Muslims (coming after 9/11 and other incidents), which made the outrageous claims more readily believed by some. The local Muslim community had little chance to counter the narrative once it began to spread widely.

- **Real-World Consequences:** Although the letter itself was **debunked as fake** early on, its effects were very real and far-reaching. Several schools in Birmingham with majority Muslim students underwent emergency inspections; staff were suspended or dismissed based on unproven allegations of extremism. Reputable schools previously rated outstanding were downgraded or put under special measures. The controversy fueled Islamophobia nationally – it **derailed the lives of thousands of young Muslim schoolchildren**, who were stigmatized by association. Many Muslim teachers and governors felt mistrusted or left the education sector due to the hostile environment created by the narrowed public perception of their identity. Policy-wise, the government imposed new requirements on schools to teach "British values," seen as a reaction to the scare. Community relations in Birmingham were strained, with some Muslims feeling under surveillance. In essence, a hoax letter sparked a witch-hunt that harmed careers and eroded community cohesion across the nation.

- **Debunking/Response:** Over time, investigative journalists and scholars exposed the truth. Local police concluded the letter was likely a fabrication with no evidence of an actual plot. By 2017, reports (e.g. in *The Guardian*) referred to the "fake 'Islamic plot'" and noted how the allegations took on a life of their own despite being unverified. A podcast investigation in 2022 (*The Trojan Horse Affair*) further cast doubt on the letter's origins and the response. The Muslim Council of Britain dubbed it the "Trojan Hoax" and called for an inquiry into how unverified info sparked such a fiasco. While officialdom never formally apologized, the initial hysteria has been widely criticized in hindsight as a case of disinformation and institutional overreaction. This episode remains a cautionary tale in the UK about the need for skepticism and fairness when sensational claims surface about minority communities.

Example 5: Brexit "Turkey Is Joining" Scare (2016, United Kingdom)

- **Target Audience:** British voters.

- **"Other":** Turkish people (and, more broadly, immigrants and Muslims, given Turkey's population is predominantly Muslim).

- **Nature of Disinformation:** During the UK's EU referendum, the pro-Brexit camp pushed a false narrative that Turkey's EU membership was imminent – and that **"Turkey (population 76 million) is joining the EU"**, with the implication that millions of Turks would soon migrate to the UK. This claim was **demonstrably false** – Turkey's accession talks were stalled and nowhere near completion. Nevertheless, Leave campaign materials presented Turkey's entry as a near-certainty. Further disinformation compounded the fear: Vote Leave released statements suggesting an influx of Turkish nationals would pose crime and security risks, citing dubious statistics about Turkish criminals. One leaflet claimed Britons would be less safe due to Turkey's high crime and gun ownership rates, and even highlighted Turkey's birthrate to project "1 million Turks to the UK by 2025". These claims were grossly misleading, playing on xenophobic fears.

- **IBD Tactics & Identity Narrowing:** This campaign used **Othering** by portraying Turks (and implicitly Muslims/immigrants) as a demographic and security threat. It employed **Emotional Manipulation** (fear of crime, uncontrolled migration, cultural change) and presented a **False Choice**: EU membership with Turkish influx vs. Brexit for safety and control. It **Promised a Narrow Identity** where British **Security**, **Agency** ("take back control"), and cultural continuity were contingent on leaving the EU and rejecting perceived threats from outsiders. This **narrowed British identity**, linking patriotism and national interest primarily to anti-immigration and anti-EU stances.

- **Spread:** Through **official campaign ads, posters, speeches, and social media.** Vote Leave and affiliated groups ran Facebook ads and distributed flyers proclaiming the Turkey assertion.   High-profile Leave politicians brought it up in interviews and debates.   For example, a prominent Leave figure (and cabinet minister) Penny Mordaunt erroneously stated on TV that the UK couldn't veto Turkey's accession – bolstering the myth that Turkey's entry was unavoidable. Tabloid newspapers also blared alarmist headlines about "Turkish migrants" and even linked the false claim to terrorism (one *Mail* article's graphic insinuated terrorists could come if Turkey joined). The message was further amplified on Twitter by Leave campaign accounts and right-wing activists, reaching a wide audience in the emotionally charged referendum environment, creating strong **Echo Chambers** for Leave voters.

- **Actors Involved:** The **Vote Leave** campaign (led by politicians) crafted and propagated these messages. The unofficial Leave.EU campaign also pushed Turkey-focused fear – unveiling a notorious "Breaking Point" poster showing Syrian refugees, implicitly conflating them with future Turkish migrants. Certain media outlets (Daily Mail, The Sun) were complicit in repeating or not challenging the false narrative. On the other side, the Remain campaign and fact-checkers did try to refute these claims, but their reach was arguably smaller. The use of dog-whistle racism (Turkey is Muslim-majority) was deliberate: it aimed to sway undecided voters by invoking latent anti-immigrant sentiments.

- **Real-World Consequences:** The Turkey disinformation contributed to **social polarization and the outcome of the Brexit vote.** Polling analysis and campaign insiders have noted that the idea of Turkey joining struck a chord among some voters worried about immigration. It bolstered the broader "take back control of our borders" theme of Leave. Ultimately, 52% voted to Leave the EU. While many factors influenced that result, the prevalence of this false claim showed how disinformation can *"divide a nation"*. In the aftermath, surveys found significant belief in the falsehood – a 2016 poll showed a large fraction of Leave voters thought Turkey was poised to join the EU. The campaign also left a legacy of mistrust: once the claims were proven untrue (after the vote, EU negotiations with Turkey remained frozen), public cynicism about politicians grew. Additionally, British Turks and Muslims felt singled out; community groups reported a spike in xenophobic comments referencing Brexit and Turkey. The UK saw a general rise in hate incidents post-referendum, partly attributed to the anti-immigrant rhetoric that had been mainstreamed by the narrowed definition of national interest.

- **Debunking/Response:** During the campaign, independent fact-checkers (e.g. BBC Reality Check, FullFact) and the Remain side repeatedly pointed out that Turkey's accession was *not* imminent – every EU member had a veto and several leaders opposed Turkey joining. Downing Street (then PM David Cameron) even stated that Turkey's membership was not on the horizon. These rebuttals, however, often came with less sensational coverage. After the referendum, the falsehood became evident: the EU formally suspended talks due to Turkey's human rights issues. Media retrospectives (e.g. *The Independent* in Dec 2017) listed the Turkey claim among the "demonstrably false" Brexit promises. A Parliamentary inquiry in 2018 into fake news highlighted the Vote Leave ads on Turkey. While no penalties were imposed for the dishonesty, these efforts at least documented the deception. The Turkey 'scare' now stands as a well-known example of referendum misinformation – serving as a warning to future political campaigns.

Example 6: Russian Trolls Fuel Racial Division (2016, United States)

- **Target Audience:** Primarily African Americans, white Americans, and other groups.

- **"Other":** Each group was sometimes positioned as the "Other" for opposing groups.

- **Nature of Disinformation:** A covert influence campaign by Russia's Internet Research Agency (IRA) spread misleading and inflammatory content about race in America. Troll-run social media accounts impersonated Black activists, spreading false or exaggerated claims of police brutality and systemic racism to heighten anger. Simultaneously, other fake accounts pushed messages to white conservatives, stoking fears of Black crime or militant activism. The trolls promulgated conspiracy theories (e.g., that the US government or "elites" were betraying whites) and fake news stories (for instance, distorted reports of incidents) to play both sides. One notorious fake persona "Blacktivist" urged African Americans that voting was useless ("our votes don't matter" – a form of voter suppression disinformation). Another account spread a false story that the NYPD officer who killed Eric Garner had been found innocent (when no verdict had occurred yet), aiming to spark outrage. The overall narrative was tailored to aggravate identity-based grievances and pit communities against each other.

- **IBD Tactics & Identity Narrowing:** This campaign masterfully used **Othering** by amplifying grievances and portraying opposing racial groups as threats or enemies to each other. It relied heavily on **Emotional Manipulation**, stoking anger, fear, resentment, and cynicism across different demographics. By creating fake personas and online groups, it **Promised a Narrow Identity** offering validation and **Belonging** within polarized echo chambers defined by racial grievance. For Black audiences, it narrowed identity towards disillusionment and disengagement (undermining agency). For white audiences, it narrowed identity towards racial anxiety and victimhood. It implicitly created **False Choices**, suggesting one must align entirely with one side of a manufactured racial conflict, thereby **narrowing identity options** and discouraging cross-racial understanding or moderate views. It exploited the need for **Justice** by twisting real issues to fuel division.

- **Spread: Social media platforms** were the main vector – Facebook, Instagram, Twitter, YouTube – via thousands of posts and ads. The Russian operatives created dozens of themed pages: "Blacktivist" on Facebook amassed over 360,000 followers, posting divisive memes daily. On Twitter, IRA accounts masqueraded as Black local news or as white nationalist users, engaging in hashtag campaigns (e.g. #Black-LivesMatter versus #BlueLivesMatter debates). They even organized real-world rallies by posting event calls – in one case, Russian trolls orchestrated simultaneous opposing protests in Houston (one by a fake Muslim group and another by a fake Texas secessionist group). Paid Facebook ads micro-targeted users: the Senate found that ads were **"principally aimed at African-Americans in key metropolitan areas"**, using location and interest targeting to maximize impact within created **Echo Chambers**. Instagram (owned by Facebook) saw a surge of IRA activity with provocative images and quotes about race. This multichannel approach ensured that divisive disinfo was widely distributed under the guise of grassroots voices.

- **Actors Involved:** The **Internet Research Agency**, a Kremlin-linked troll farm based in St. Petersburg, Russia, master-minded this operation. Dozens of IRA staff ("trolls") managed fake accounts around the clock. They stole profile photos, invented personas (often using American-sounding names), and interacted with unwitting real users. The Russian government was the ultimate actor behind it, as later confirmed by U.S. intelligence. U.S. social media companies were the unwitting facilitators; their algorithms sometimes boosted the most divisive content. Eventually, Twitter, Facebook, and others helped identify and shut down these accounts – but not until after the campaign had run rampant for at least two years.

- **Real-World Consequences:** The campaign successfully **exacerbated social polarization**. While it's hard to quantify its effect on voting, a U.S. Senate report noted the IRA had an "overwhelming operational emphasis on race" and that no group was targeted more than African Americans. The content aimed to depress Black voter turnout (by sowing cynicism about voting) and simultaneously energize conservative whites with fear-mongering, arguably contributing to the divisive climate around the 2016 election. It also led to real-world disruption: actual protests organized by fake accounts did occur (often small, but they demonstrated the trolls' ability to mobilize Americans on opposite sides of an issue to literally face off on the street). The disinformation likely deepened mistrust between racial communities and towards institutions, a direct result of the successful narrowing and polarization of identities. For example, some African American voters became more convinced the system was rigged against them, while some whites were pushed further into alt-right conspiracy thinking. Even after the election, Russia kept fueling racial discord – IRA content on race spiked again in 2017-2018, including around events like the Charlottesville rally. The lasting consequence is an American public more aware yet also more entrenched in polarized narratives about race, some of which were artificially amplified by foreign disinformation.

- **Debunking/Response:** U.S. intelligence agencies and investigative journalists began exposing the IRA operations in late 2017. In 2018 13 Russian individuals and the IRA organization were indicted for fraud and interference, detailing their tactics. Social media companies, under pressure, released data: Facebook admitted the Russian content reached millions, and the Senate Intelligence Committee commissioned independent analyses (e.g. by Oxford University/Graphika) which published reports in 2018. These reports thoroughly debunked the IRA narratives by revealing their source and intent. They showed how accounts like "Woke Blacks" specifically urged Black citizens to abstain from voting. Once unmasked, the faux activism lost credibility and the accounts were suspended. Civil society groups like the **ADL** and academia continue to monitor and publicize racist disinformation campaigns.

Example 7: "Great Replacement" Conspiracy Theory (2010s–present, Western countries)

- **Target Audience:** Primarily white Europeans/North Americans.

- **"Other":** Immigrant groups (Muslims, Africans, Jews, etc.).

- **Nature of Disinformation:** The "Great Replacement" is a **white nationalist conspiracy theory** claiming that white populations are being intentionally replaced by non-white immigrants through mass migration and demographic growth. Proponents allege a secret plan by elites (often implicating Jews or leftist governments) to dilute or destroy white European culture by encouraging immigration from Africa, the Middle East, and Asia. This narrative is not based in fact – it twists demographic trends into a sinister plot. The disinformation often includes fake statistics or alarmist misinterpretations (e.g., "Europe will be 50% Muslim by 2050" – not supported by real data). It also frequently features **racist tropes**: depicting immigrants as invaders, rapists, or criminals, and asserting that declining white birth rates are orchestrated. In the U.S., a variant claims Democrats are importing immigrants to "replace" white voters – a notion echoed in phrases like "white genocide." This theory, once fringe, has been debunked but has spread widely in far-right circles.

- **IBD Tactics & Identity Narrowing:** This theory is built on extreme **Othering** (immigrants/minorities as existential threats, often linked to anti-Semitic tropes about elites). It uses powerful **Emotional Manipulation**, stoking existential fear ("replacement," "white genocide"), paranoia, anger, and resentment. It **Promises a Narrow Identity** where white **Security**, **Continuity** (cultural/racial lineage), **Self-Esteem** (as defenders), and **Belonging** (within white nationalist groups) are achievable *only* by embracing a racially defined identity based on victimhood and opposition to diversity. This drastically **narrows white identity**, demanding rejection of multiculturalism, empathy, and shared humanity with non-white groups. It presents a **False Choice**: resist "replacement" (often violently) or face extinction.

- **Spread:** Initially propagated in **far-right books and online**

forums, it has since spread via social media, meme culture, and even mainstream political rhetoric. French writer Renaud Camus popularized "Le Grand Remplacement" in a 2011 book, and the idea spread on platforms like 4chan, 8chan, and alt-right websites. White supremacist groups (Generation Identity in Europe, etc.) created slick propaganda – YouTube videos, Facebook groups – around the theme. Marchers in Charlottesville in 2017 chanted "You will not replace us," a direct reference to the theory. On Twitter and Facebook, thousands of posts (often using coded language or referring to immigration headlines) spread the meme of an ongoing "replacement." Some politicians and news outlets in Europe and the U.S. gave it legitimacy. The theory has also been shared in Telegram channels and local right-wing newsletters, constantly adapting to news (e.g., during the 2015 refugee crisis or 2021 U.S. border surge, "replacement" talk spiked), reinforcing belief within **Echo Chambers**.

- **Actors Involved:** Key actors include **far-right ideologues and extremist communities**. White nationalist and identitarian groups actively push this theory as a core justification for their movements. Individuals like Renaud Camus (France) or Richard Spencer (U.S.) acted as early advocates. In recent years, elements of mainstream right-wing politics and media have flirted with or endorsed the narrative. Additionally, the theory circulates organically among online followers who produce content (memes, YouTube commentary). Notably, multiple terrorist shooters effectively became actors propagating the theory by citing it in manifestos – giving the conspiracy global attention. On the opposing side, anti-hate organizations (ADL, SPLC) and fact-checkers act to counter it, but their reach in the echo chambers of the far-right is limited.

- **Real-World Consequences:** Though entirely unfounded, the "Great Replacement" disinformation has **inspired real-world violence and policy shifts**. It has been explicitly cited by at least three mass murderers: the Christchurch, New Zealand shooter (2019) titled his manifesto "The Great Replacement," justifying the massacre of 51 Muslims at mosques as a defense of the white race. The El Paso shooter (2019) who killed 23 in a Texas Walmart targeting Hispanics also referenced a "Hispanic invasion" replacing white Americans. In 2022, a gunman in Buffalo targeted Black shoppers, killing 10, after posting a manifesto steeped in replacement theory. These tragedies show how an internet conspiracy fueled by narrowed identity and hatred translated into terror. Beyond violence, the theory has contributed to polarization and anti-immigrant policies. For example, it arguably influenced stricter anti-refugee stances in Europe (politicians invoking "population replacement" to block asylum seekers). In France, it fueled anti-Muslim sentiment; in the U.S., it has become a part of the nativist rhetoric opposing immigration and even justified attempts at voter suppression (under the guise of preventing a "replacement" of the electorate). For communities of color, Jews, and immigrants, this disinformation fosters an atmosphere of fear – hate crimes and harassment have risen where such ideas gain traction. Society-wide, it erodes social cohesion by casting diversity as an existential threat.

- **Debunking/Response: Experts and media have repeatedly debunked the Great Replacement theory**. Demographers point out that immigration in Western countries is a complex phenomenon, not a malicious plot, and that no evidence supports a secret plan to "replace" anyone. Fact-checkers clarify that while demographics shift over time, the theory's core claim of a deliberate eradication of whites is false and rooted in racist ideology. After the Buffalo shooting, even U.S. mainstream outlets (NPR, NYT) did explain how replacement theory is baseless yet dangerous. Social media platforms have taken mixed action – some outright white nationalist expressions are banned, but coded references still circulate. Counter-speech campaigns by civil rights groups have tried to educate the public. For instance, the **Southern Poverty Law Center** and **Institute for Strategic Dialogue** have published explainers labeling the theory as a hateful conspiracy with no factual grounding. In some countries, embracing this theory has backfired politically when opponents call it out (e.g., when a French far-right politician explicitly mentioned "replacement," it drew widespread criticism). While the narrative persists in extremist echo chambers, public awareness that it's disinformation has grown. Notably, conservative leaders in the U.S. and Europe have been pressed by media to disavow the theory. The struggle continues, but many view the "Great Replacement" as a prime example of modern identity-based disinformation.

Example 8: Incel Misogynistic Narratives (2010s–present, online subculture)

- **Target Audience:** Young men struggling with social isolation or romantic rejection.

- **"Other":** Women (as a group, especially sexually active women, feminists, etc.).

- **Nature of Disinformation:** "Incel" (involuntary celibate) communities propagate a range of false and misogynistic claims about women and society. Central to incel ideology is the **disinformation** that feminism and sexual liberation have created a rigged system where only a few men get all the partners, while average men are doomed to loneliness. They assert as fact that women are shallow, hypergamous (only choosing the top 20% of attractive men) – an **unfounded idea** often "supported" by distorted pseudo-scientific arguments about looks and evolution. Incels frequently claim that women inherently despise or ignore "nice guys," which is presented as a conspiracy against them. Extreme incel posts describe women as less than human, or as property that men are unjustly denied. One prevalent false narrative is that society gives women excessive sexual power ("feminism has given women power over sex and romance"), which incels believe is used to oppress certain men. These narratives are steeped in confirmation bias and misogyny, not actual data about relationships. They also deny the agency of women (e.g., claiming women only exist to mate with alpha males). Incel ideology thus constitutes disinformation about gender relations – a warped picture of reality that justifies hatred.

- **IBD Tactics & Identity Narrowing:** Incel ideology employs extreme **Othering** (dehumanizing women, demonizing successful men/"Chads") and intense **Emotional Manipulation** (fueling despair, self-pity, anger, resentment). It **Promises a Narrow Identity** defined entirely by perceived sexual failure and victimhood. This **drastically narrows the identity** of young men, discouraging personal growth, social connection outside the group, and healthy views of relationships. It offers **Belonging** within a toxic online community and a perverse sense of **Significance** through shared grievance and ideology (the "black pill"). It creates **False Choices** (Chad vs. Incel, Stacy vs. worthless) and undermines agency by promoting fatalism ("it's over") or misdirecting it towards violence.

- **Spread: Online forums and social media** are the incubators of incel narratives. On message boards like 4chan (/r9k/), 8chan, and dedicated incel forums (such as the now-defunct Incels.me), users share memes, fake "statistics," and anecdotal "proof" of their claims. Reddit housed incel communities ("/r/Incels" and later "/r/Braincels") until they were banned, and these had tens of thousands of members. Incels also spread their ideas via YouTube channels and comment sections – some self-proclaimed incel vloggers produce rant videos citing evolutionary psychology (often misinterpreted) to "explain" why women are evil or why only looks matter. Twitter and TikTok occasionally see incel-style content or hashtags (though such content often gets moderated if overt). The manosphere at large (men's rights blogs, pickup artist sites) can act as a gateway; incel ideas evolved partially from pickup artist forums gone sour. Recommendation algorithms sometimes funnel lonely young men from innocuous self-help or fitness content into incel or extremist misogynistic content. The spread is transnational (incel forums include users from North America, Europe, South Asia, etc., all communicating in English and sharing the same memes and jargon like "red pill," "black pill," "Stacy" for attractive women, etc.).   The COVID lockdowns saw some uptick in online incel activity. These forums act as powerful **Echo Chambers**.

- **Actors Involved:**   Unlike state-sponsored disinformation, incel narratives are spread by a **loosely organized online subculture**. Key actors are influential incel forum users and moderators who set the tone. Certain individuals known as incel "ideologues" write lengthy posts or manifestos – for instance, an infamous user named "foreveralone" compiled distorted "research" that is often cited within the community. Outside the forums, some far-right or alt-right figures also amplify incel-adjacent ideas (there is overlap with white supremacist and male supremacist movements). No central authority propagates incel beliefs; it's a self-reinforcing ecosystem. Tech platforms inadvertently acted as enablers by giving them space until policy changes (Reddit banned incels for hate speech in 2017, YouTube has removed some extreme channels). In some cases, **violent actors** have taken these narratives offline – e.g., Elliot Rodger (2014 Isla Vista shooter) and Alek Minassian (2018 Toronto van attacker) both posted manifestos echoing incel disinformation about women before committing murder.   These perpetrators then become martyrs or "saints" in incel lore, which further spreads the ideology.

- **Real-World Consequences:** Incel disinformation has fueled **hatred and violence against women**. Since 2014, self-identified incels have killed over 50 people (mostly women) in North America. High-profile cases: Elliot Rodger killed 6 in California (targeting women in a sorority and men he perceived as rivals) after spewing misogynistic conspiracy theories in a video; Alek Minassian's van attack killed 10 in Toronto, predominantly women, as he explicitly sought "revenge" for incels. There have been at least four lethal attacks in Canada tied to incel ideology, leading Canadian intelligence to classify **violent misogyny as a form of extremist terrorism**. Beyond these tragedies, incel rhetoric contributes to everyday harassment of women – online mob attacks on female journalists, gamers (e.g., Gamergate had incel-like elements), and even random women being doxxed or threatened by forum users. It can also negatively affect young men's mental health: instead of seeking productive help for social issues, men in these forums are steeped in despair and anger, sometimes encouraging each other towards self-harm or suicide. The narratives increase gender polarization – fostering distrust and reinforcing harmful stereotypes, a direct result of the severely narrowed identity promoted by the ideology. In sum, these false narratives have translated into both lethal violence and a toxic online environment that undermines gender equality and public safety.

- **Debunking/Response:** Countering incel disinformation is challenging because it's intertwined with personal grievances. However, several steps have been taken: Major platforms have shut down incel groups (Reddit's ban, Discord bans, etc.), dispersing some of the audience. Researchers and psychologists actively publish **refutations of incel claims** – for example, data showing most people (men and women) eventually find partners, contradicting the "80/20 rule" myth. Feminist groups and educators try to engage young men with factual sex education and discussions about consent and relationships, to preempt the allure of incel ideology. Some former incels have spoken out, debunking the movement's tenets from personal experience. There are also online communities focused on **"incel exit" or support**, which offer empathy and encourage men to seek therapy rather than blame women. In the media, documentaries and articles have shed light on the fallacies of incel logic, often quoting experts: e.g., sociologists explaining that incels vastly overestimate how "selective" women are, and that the claims of looks being the only factor are not true. Law enforcement now monitors incel forums due to the violence risk, and at times intervenes – for instance, a planned incel attack in Ohio was thwarted by the FBI in 2020. While not a traditional fact-check scenario, the response to incel disinformation is a mix of **deplatforming, education, and addressing the underlying social issues** (like loneliness and misogyny) that fuel the narrative. The goal is to expose that incel claims are toxic distortions, and to steer those affected towards healthier worldviews about themselves and women.

Example 9: Anti-LGBT "Gender Ideology" Myth – Colombia Peace Referendum (2016, Colombia)

- **Target Audience:** Conservative and religious Colombians.

- **"Other":** LGBTQ+ individuals and proponents of gender equality in Colombia.

- **Nature of Disinformation:** In 2016, Colombia held a referendum to ratify a peace accord with the FARC rebels. A wave of disinformation alleged the peace deal sneaked in a sinister **"gender ideology"** agenda. Critics falsely claimed the accord would impose LGBTQ indoctrination, undermine "family values," and even mandate pro-LGBT education in schools. For example, a line in an *unrelated* draft education guide ("One isn't born a man or woman, but learns to be one…") was circulated out of context and labeled as proof of a radical agenda. **False versions of documents** were spread on social media, asserting that the peace agreement would allow children to choose their gender or legalize same-sex adoption (in fact, those issues were not dictated by the accord). Conservatives branded it an attack on Christian morals – a complete distortion since the actual accord's gender provisions simply aimed to ensure women's and minorities' inclusion (e.g., acknowledging sexual violence issues, assuring reintegration benefits applied equally). The term "gender ideology" itself was a bogeyman – painting any gender/sexuality equality measure as a nefarious doctrine. In reality, the accusations were myths with no basis in the actual text.

- **IBD Tactics & Identity Narrowing:** This campaign used **Othering** by framing LGBTQ+ rights and gender equality as a dangerous, foreign "ideology." It employed **Emotional Manipulation**, stoking fear (threat to children, family, religion) and moral panic among conservative/religious voters. It **Promised a Narrow Identity** where **Security** (of traditional values) and continuity (of faith/family structures) were linked to rejecting the peace deal. This created a **False Choice** between supporting peace and upholding traditional/religious values, effectively **narrowing the identity** of conservative Colombians by making these seem mutually exclusive. **Belonging** within religious communities was leveraged to mobilize opposition based on these fears.

- **Spread:** The misinformation spread via **social networks (Facebook, WhatsApp)** and crucially through church networks. Prominent evangelical and Catholic leaders warned congregations about "gender ideology" in sermons and WhatsApp blasts. By August 2016, massive protests were organized against an education ministry's sexuality handbook (falsely tied to the peace deal). These networks acted as powerful **Echo Chambers**, rapidly disseminating the fear-based narrative among receptive audiences. Political opponents of the peace deal also amplified the claims.

- **Actors Involved:** Conservative political figures (notably former President Álvaro Uribe and his party), evangelical and some Catholic church leaders, and associated social media activists were key actors. They deliberately conflated the peace accord's gender provisions with unrelated controversies to mobilize their base against the referendum. The campaign manager for the "No" vote later admitted they focused on stoking "indignation" rather than explaining the deal.

- **Real-World Consequences:** The "No" vote narrowly won the referendum (50.2% to 49.8%), derailing the initial peace agreement (though a revised version was later implemented). Analysts widely agree the "gender ideology" disinformation played a significant role in mobilizing conservative voters against the deal. It **deepened social polarization** around gender and sexuality issues, making dialogue more difficult. LGBTQ+ individuals faced increased stigma and hostility. The episode demonstrated how IBD targeting cultural anxieties (needs for **Security** and **Continuity**) can sway political outcomes and damage social cohesion by successfully **narrowing identity** and creating false dichotomies.

- **Debunking/Response:** Supporters of the peace deal, human rights groups, and some media outlets attempted to debunk the "gender ideology" claims, explaining the actual (modest) gender provisions in the accord. They pointed out the conflation with unrelated issues and the lack of evidence for the fear-mongering narratives. However, these rational explanations struggled to compete with the emotionally charged disinformation spreading through trusted religious and social networks (the **Echo Chambers**). After the referendum loss, the government and FARC renegotiated parts of the accord, slightly modifying some gender language to appease critics, but the core principles remained. The incident highlighted the challenge of countering IBD when it taps into deeply held cultural and religious identities and leverages the power of **Belonging** within those groups.

5 The Power of Positive Identity Expansion: Our Strategy

While identity-based disinformation seeks to divide and narrow our sense of self, we possess a powerful, proactive strategy to counter its effects: **Positive Identity Expansion**. This chapter delves into this evidence-based approach, showing how we can build resilience and reclaim our narratives not by directly fighting the negativity, but by actively cultivating the richness and diversity within our own identities and communities.

The Power of Positive Identity Expansion

The effectiveness of positive identity expansion is supported by a wealth of academic research from different disciplines, as detailed in the chapter, 'Academic Research Supporting the Toolkit'.

For now, it is sufficient to understand that this approach is defined by four central principles:

Meeting Underlying Needs

Positive Identity Expansion addresses the same needs that IBD exploits (belonging, self-esteem, etc.), but does so in a way that doesn't force the target audience down narrow false choices and 'us'/'them' thinking. Instead, we show that these needs can be met through a celebration of community and cultural/ethnic/religious heritage and participation, and through an acknowledgement of the richness and complexity of our individual and group identities.

Broadening, Not Narrowing

Again, Identity-Based Disinformation tries to shrink or reduce identity expression; in this approach, we set out to expand it. We remind people of the full range of their options to express their values, beliefs, and experiences. We show and celebrate that seemingly conflicting ideas do actually coexist within a healthy identity. For example, you can be both patriotic and critical of your country's flaws. You can be deeply religious and also support scientific progress.

Celebrating Diversity

As above, we highlight the richness and diversity of the target audience's culture and heritage. We celebrate the many different ways people express (and have expressed in the past) their identities. This requires moving beyond surface-level observations to understand the deep cultural, traditional, religious, and historical contexts that shape the audience's worldview and values.

Building Resilience

A strong, diverse, and inclusive sense of identity acts like a shield against disinformation. If you have a strong sense of who you are, based on a wide range of values and experiences, you're less likely to be influenced by manipulative IBD messaging.

Why Direct Confrontation Often Doesn't Work

It might seem natural to fight bad information with facts and arguments. However, research shows that directly confronting or debunking identity-based disinformation (IBD) can be ineffective or even backfire.

One reason for this is that when someone attacks a belief that's tied to our sense of who we are, our first instinct is often to defend it, not question it. Challenging core beliefs can feel like a personal attack, leading people to dig in their heels even more, regardless of the evidence presented.

Experts in communication and conflict resolution often advise against confrontational approaches when individuals are already under the influence of identity-based disinformation. For instance, the OPPATTUNE Methods Handbook 2025 stresses the need for non-confrontational dialogue, focusing on understanding rather than arguing. Similarly, research on reducing prejudice (Yabanci, 2024) found that sharing positive, alternative stories was far more effective than direct debate (see Chapter, Academic Research Supporting the Toolkit).

Furthermore, insights from organizations like the OICD (creators of this toolkit) suggest that direct confrontation to those under the influence of IBD is often ineffective because these individuals may feel they have few other ways to meet their core needs than taking on the versions of self on offer by the IBD. Attacking the narrative they cling to simply risks positioning the confronter as just another threat, reinforcing the 'us vs. them' dynamic that the IBD thrives upon and making release from its influence even more challenging as a result.

This doesn't mean facts and critical thinking aren't important. Confronting mis- and disinformation of all kinds with facts is a vital part of the effort to counter and prevent their harmful effects. However, for many individuals and communities already under the influence of Identity-Based Disinformation, an approach which more subtly prepares the ground for facts to be introduced and absorbed is appropriate. Positive Identity Expansion lays that groundwork by providing alternative ways to express core needs, providing access to new expressive options, and helping the target audience to overcome false choices.

By successfully implementing the positive approach that is at the heart of this toolkit, you will provide the conditions for facts and critical thinking to enter back into circulation. By ensuring that these diverse alternative narratives are in circulation, you will also increase resilience against future IBD campaigns.

Reframing "Counter-Narratives" as " 'Equal' Alternative Narratives"

There is a long history of trying to confront dangerous IBD with messages which challenge them and provide a direct "counter narrative": a story or message which reverses or flips the logic, 'truth', and moral position of the narrative it is countering. Taken literally, a counter narrative simply says "your narrative is wrong/false: the truth (or 'right' way) is [the opposite]".

In practice, counter narratives may be more sophisticated than a direct attempt to flip the legitimacy of the IBD narrative and present an opposite. Certainly, when trying to counter IBD using Positive Identity Expansion, we require a 'counter narrative' which doesn't try to overtly reverse or delegitimize the IBD at all. Instead, we want a narrative which resonates with the audience for whom the IBD resonates - not one which says to them "what you are supporting or believing in is invalid or wrong".

This shift from confronting to resonating prompts us to refine our understanding of the type of narrative we are seeking to put into circulation.

The term "Equal Alternative Narratives" is a more suited to our Positive Identity Expansion approach for the following important reasons:

Meeting Needs, Not Just Opposing

The core of our strategy is to be at least *equally effective* in meeting the underlying human needs that the IBD exploits (belonging, self-esteem, security, etc.). Of course, instead of using those needs to narrow identities and force an 'us'/'them' version of reality, our approach is to offer *alternative* ways to fulfill these needs which celebrate positive senses of self.

Proactive, Not Reactive

We are not simply reacting to the IBD; we are proactively building a stronger foundation where people have greater choice and control over the representations they use (also called promoting narrative/identity agency).

Emphasis on Out-Competing

Our narratives seek to compete with the IBD: i.e. be *at least equally* compelling, equally fulfilling of needs, equally psychologically resonant, and ultimately, of course, *more* effective in allowing the individual to choose alternative ways to express themselves than those the IBD dictates.

Focus on Alternatives

The term "alternative" obviously emphasizes that we are providing different options, different ways of understanding the world and one's place within it. We are expanding the range of possibilities, not limiting them.

Avoiding the "Backfire Effect"

By framing our approach as "equal alternative narratives", we avoid the common trap of directly confronting the IBD with the 'binary opposite' counter narrative, which can readily backfire. We are offering a different path, but not attempting to force an individual to take it (unlike IBD which attempts to manipulate the availability of narratives through triggering fear and other needs).

Core Principles of Equal Alternative Narratives

- **Positive**: We focus on building up, not tearing down

- **Proactive**: We are creating a positive vision, not just reacting to negativity

- **Empowering**: We offer choices and expand possibilities

- **Needs-Based**: We address underlying human needs in a healthy way

- **Choice-Based**: We do not manipulate the availability of narratives (like the IBD), but merely offer alternatives which resonate

- **Resilient**: We build a stronger foundation that is less susceptible to manipulation

Crucial Clarification: The term "equal" here refers *specifically* to the aim of matching and seeking to outcompete the **psychological effectiveness** and **need-fulfillment capacity** of the IBD narrative for the target audience. It **does not** imply any moral, ethical, or factual equivalence between the positive alternative and the potentially harmful IBD. The strategic goal is to create alternatives that are *equally compelling* on a psychological level, thereby providing a viable, positive pathway for the audience.

Key Principle: Focus on the Target Audience not the 'Other'

Another key principle of the Positive Identity Expansion approach may seem counterintuitive at first: We produce equal alternative narratives as a resource for use by the *target audience* of the IBD; NOT as a resource to (directly) assist the 'other' group that may appear in the IBD (although of course we expect that if our alternative narratives are successful, the 'other' will be less likely suffer attacks - and this could of course be our ultimate goal).

Understanding Our Focus

- **Target Audience**: The group of people the IBD creators are trying to influence. They are the ones receiving the manipulative messages - *the targets of the IBD's manipulative tactics.*

- **"Others"**: The individuals or groups being attacked or demonized in the disinformation.

In conventional disinformation counter messaging, we may well feel compelled, (with good reason), to want to directly assist the 'other' group who are 'under attack'. The Positive Identity Expansion approach sees that it is the *target audience* that is the primary target of the IBD attempts to inflict harm through psychological (identity-based) manipulation. By focusing on the individuals whose identities are being narrowed *in order* for the 'other' group to be perceived as 'the other', or, 'the enemy', this approach attempts to address the 'cause' and not 'the symptom' of the intended harm.

The goal of a Positive Identity Expansion approach is thus to strengthen the target audience's sense of self, providing access to resonant positive narratives that act as an off-ramp and shield against the IBD's influence. We do this by focusing exclusively on promoting positive values, building connections, and fostering understanding within the target audience, and NOT by setting out to defend against or reverse the negative representations of the 'other'.

Important Note

We never use the Positive Identity Expansion approach to criticize or attack *anyone* or stretch or bend its key principles as outlined in this chapter. We ensure we are only ever creating new (or reintroducing existing/forgotten) equal alternative narratives (identity options) for the target audience.

A Note on Intra-Group Division

It's important to recognize that IBD doesn't always pit one distinct community against another (inter-group). Sometimes, campaigns aim to create divisions *within* a larger group (intra-group) by targeting specific sub-groups and manipulating them to view other sub-groups within their own community as the 'Other'. Examples include attempts to divide different factions within a political movement, different generations within an ethnic group, or different sects within a religion (as seen in some historical examples like the Russian trolls targeting sub-groups within the Black community).

Even in these complex cases, the core principle of this toolkit remains the same: identify the specific sub-group being targeted for manipulation (the Target Audience for that specific IBD message) and focus on expanding *their* identity options and resilience through positive narratives relevant to them, rather than primarily focusing on defending the sub-group being positioned as the 'Other'. The goal is always to strengthen the resilience of those being manipulated.

6 Implementation Steps: A Step-by-Step Guide

In this chapter, we detail the steps for implementing the Reclaiming Our Narrative approach. Worksheets and AI Prompts are provided to assist each step at the back of this guide. In the chapter which follows this one, we demonstrate how these implementation steps can be applied to a real world case study. We recommend cross-referral to these sections of the guide as you absorb the techniques of each of the steps presented here.

Step 1: Analyze the IBD Campaign

The first step of the process is to carefully examine the disinformation campaign that we are attempting to redress. Understanding what messages are being spread and how they operate will help identify who is being targeted and the nature of the attempted IBD manipulation, its tactics and techniques.

Gather Examples

Collect examples of the IBD messages. This could include:

- Social media posts (screenshots, links)

- Articles or blog posts

- Memes

- Videos

- Conversations you've heard or been engaged in

Pro Tip: Try to gather examples from diverse sources (online platforms, community discussions, different media outlets) to get a broader picture of the IBD narrative and its variations.

Identify the Themes

Look for recurring themes and patterns in the messages. What are the main ideas being pushed?

- Example: "Immigrants are taking our jobs." "The government is trying to control us." "Traditional values are under attack."

Identify the Emotions

What emotions are the messages trying to evoke?

- Positive Emotions: Pride, belonging, hope, relief

- Negative Emotions: Fear, anger, resentment, insecurity, distrust, disgust

Needs Analysis

For each IBD message, identify which fundamental human needs it's targeting and how it promises to fulfill these needs:

1. **Belonging and Love**

- Description: The need to feel connected to others, to be part of a group that accepts and values you. This includes family bonds, friendships, romantic relationships, community ties, religious, political, ethnic, cultural and national affiliations.

- Analysis Questions:
    - Is the IBD promising greater belonging to a group by adopting certain beliefs or joining a particular movement?

    - Does it suggest that the target audience will be rejected or isolated from a group if they don't align with certain views?

    - What emotions are evoked when this need is manipulated (e.g., fear of rejection, comfort in group acceptance)?

2. **Self-Esteem, Status & Significance**

- Description: The need to feel valued, valid and worthy. This includes the desire for recognition, respect, achievement, and a sense that your life has meaning and purpose.

- Analysis Questions:
    - How does the IBD promise to enhance the target audience's self-esteem or status?

    - Does it suggest that certain beliefs or actions will

make them more significant or respected?

- What emotions are triggered when this need is manipulated (e.g., pride, validation, fear of insignificance)?

3. **Equality & Justice**

- Description: The need to feel that you are treated fairly, that there is balance in society, and that wrongs can be righted. This includes concerns about fairness, rights, and equitable treatment.

- Analysis Questions:
  - Does the IBD frame certain situations as unjust or unfair to the target audience?

  - Does it promise to restore justice or a power balance by supporting certain views or groups and demonizing or attacking others?

  - What emotions emerge when this need is manipulated (e.g., indignation, righteousness, desire for retribution)?

4. **Freedom from Fear and Suffering (Security)**

- Description: The need to feel safe, protected, and free from threats. This includes physical safety, economic security, health, and the stability of one's way of life.

- Analysis Questions:

- How does the IBD amplify or create fears about the target audience's security?

- Does it promise protection or safety if certain views are adopted?

- What emotions are provoked when this need is manipulated (e.g., anxiety, relief, gratitude toward "protectors")?

Identify Identity Manipulation

How is the IBD trying to shape the target audience's sense of self? What narrow version of their identity is being promoted? What aspects are being suppressed or discredited?

- Example: The IBD might be trying to convince people that they can only be "true patriots" if they support a particular political party or hold certain views. It might be trying to discredit people who are both religious and environmentally conscious.

Identify False Choices

Look for "either/or" statements that force a false choice.

- Example: "You have to choose between your faith and science." "You can't be a loyal citizen and also criticize the government."

Analyze Power Dynamics

Explicitly consider how power imbalances might be influencing the IBD campaign:

- **Identify Power Holders:** Who holds significant societal power (political, economic, social, media) relevant to this context? Consider the senders of the IBD, the target audience, and any 'othered' groups.

- **Assess Resource Disparities:** Are there noticeable differences in resources (funding, media access, networks) between those spreading the IBD and those potentially affected or trying to counter it?

- **Consider Influence on Narrative:** How might existing power structures make the IBD narrative seem more credible or harder to challenge? Does it align with or reinforce narratives already promoted by powerful actors?

- **Impact on Reach and Reception:** How could power dynamics affect who sees the IBD and how they interpret it? Are certain channels dominated by specific power groups?

Incorporating this analysis helps create a more realistic understanding of the IBD's context and potential impact.

Write it Down

Summarize your analysis of the IBD campaign. Use the included worksheet at the end of this guide to help create a structured document that includes:

- Main themes and narratives

- Emotions being evoked

- Needs being targeted and how they're being manipulated

- Identity manipulation tactics

- False choices being presented

- Power dynamics in force

- Specific examples that illustrate each of these elements

This comprehensive analysis will serve as the foundation for developing your equal-alternative narrative strategy in the next steps.

Use the implementation case study in the next chapter, the worksheets and AI prompts at the end of this guide to help you complete the IBD analysis.

Pro Tip: When analyzing needs, focus on the *receiver's perspective*. Ask: "What need does believing or sharing this message to fulfill for *them*?" Put yourself in the target audiences' shoes and imagine how the IBD narrative could appeal to you in that context. It can be easier to proceed through step 2 below before returning to this step again to achieve a greater empathy with the target audience.

Step 2: Define and Understand Your Target Audience

Now that you understand the IBD campaign itself, the next step is to deeply understand your target audience. Remember that your target audience is NOT the group being attacked by the IBD, but rather the group being influenced to adopt narrow identity positions.

Use the included worksheet and AI prompt at the end of this guide to assist you and refer to the next chapter's real world case study implementation example.

Comprehensive Audience Analysis

- **Core Demographics**

    - Age Composition: What age ranges are most affected? Consider different generational experiences and values.

    - Geographic Context: Where do they live? Consider urban/rural differences, regional cultural variations, and local history.

    - Cultural Background: What are their cultural, ethnic, religious, and linguistic backgrounds? Look for diversity within these categories.

    - Socioeconomic Factors: Consider income levels, types of employment, education levels, and economic concerns.

- **Identity Ecosystem**

    - Identity Layers: What are the multiple identities held by this audience? (e.g., professional, religious, cultural, familial, regional)

    - Identity Hierarchy: Which identity aspects are most salient or valued in different contexts?

    - Identity Tensions: Where do they experience pressure or

conflict between different aspects of identity?

- Identity Evolution: How have their collective identities changed over time? What aspects have remained constant?

• **Psychological Profile**

- Core Values: What principles guide their decisions and worldview? (e.g., family, tradition, freedom, security, progress)

- Fundamental Needs: Which psychological needs are most important to them? (belonging, self-esteem, security, meaning)

- Pain Points: What concerns, anxieties, or threats do they perceive to their identity and way of life?

- Aspirations: What are their hopes for themselves, their families, and their communities?

• **Information Landscape**

- Trust Networks: Who do they consider credible and trustworthy sources of information?

- Digital Presence: Which platforms, online communities, and media channels do they engage with regularly?

- Information Consumption: How do they typically receive and process information? (formats, timing, context)

- Social Influencers: Which community leaders, public figures, or everyday individuals shape their perspectives?

Research Methods for Target Audience Understanding

- **Direct Engagement**

  - Informal Conversations: Engage with community members in natural settings

  - Community Events: Attend gathering places where the target audience congregates

  - Active Listening: Pay attention to recurring themes, concerns, and values expressed. This involves trying to see the world through their eyes (an "emic" perspective), understanding *why* certain narratives resonate.

  - Collaborative Consultation: Wherever possible, engage in dialogue *with* members of the target audience (this might include your own friends, family, or network if they are part of this group) to understand their perspectives directly. This is key to capturing the "ordinary ways" IBD attempts to represent their needs and worldview.

- **Digital Ethnography**

  - Platform Observation: Observe (without engaging)

community discussions in online spaces

- Content Analysis: Study popular content, shared articles, and discussions

- Language Patterns: Note specific terminology, expressions, and communication styles

- **Historical Context**

  - Community History: Research significant historical
  events that shaped local identity

  - Cultural Traditions: Understand traditional practices
  and their evolution over time

  - Media Representation: Review how the community has
  been portrayed in media

Pro Tip: Go beyond surface demographics. Understanding core
values, identity tensions, and trusted information sources is often
more crucial than just knowing age or location. Use methods like
informal conversations and observing online discussions to uncover
these deeper insights.

Audience Archetype Development

After gathering information, create a detailed audience archetype
that includes:

- **Primary Archetype Description**

  Create a rich, nuanced portrait of your target audience. For
  example:

"Rural families (primarily ages 35-65) in the Eastern Tennessee region with multi-generational roots in the area. Many work in industries facing economic transition (manufacturing, mining, agriculture) and have strong ties to local churches and community organizations. They value self-reliance, family bonds, and cultural traditions while navigating economic uncertainties. They receive information primarily through local Facebook groups, regional news outlets, and community networks. Their identity includes strong regional pride, religious faith, and familial roles, with tensions between preserving traditional ways of life and adapting to economic and social changes."

- **Audience Variation Notes**

Acknowledge diversity within your target audience. For example:

"While the primary archetype represents the core audience, there are important variations to consider:

- Younger members (18-34) who remain in the community but have more digital connectivity and exposure to outside influences

- Those with different levels of religious involvement, from deeply devout to culturally religious

- Economic diversity, from struggling financially to relatively secure middle-class status

- Varying degrees of connection to urban centers and external cultural influences"

- **Vulnerability Assessment**

Identify specific vulnerabilities that IBD might exploit:

"This audience is particularly vulnerable to narratives that:

  - Frame economic challenges as deliberate attacks on their way of life

  - Position traditional values as under threat from outside forces

  - Create false choices between maintaining cultural identity and embracing change

  - Exploit feelings of being overlooked or disrespected by mainstream institutions"

- **Documentation and Application**

Create a detailed audience profile document (use the worksheet to help if needed) that:

  - Synthesizes all research findings

  - Highlights key identity components and their relationships

  - Identifies specific vulnerabilities to IBD

  - Outlines authentic communication channels and trusted voices

 – Includes concrete examples of language, cultural references, and values

This comprehensive understanding will serve as the foundation for
all subsequent steps, ensuring your equal alternative narratives genuinely resonate with and serve the needs of your target audience.

Remember: The more deeply you understand your audience, the
more effectively you can create narratives that expand their identity
options rather than narrowing them.

**Use the implementation case study in the next chapter and the
worksheets and AI prompts at the end of this guide to help you
complete this step.**

Action Point: Ensure your audience analysis captures not just
demographics but also the deep cultural context – core stories,
traditions, historical narratives, and cultural/ethnic/religious
frameworks influencing their worldview.

Relevant OICD Resources

Visit oicd.net/resources to access the latest resources including:

- **Understanding Culture in Stories: A Handbook of Methods
  for Practitioners**

  – Six evidence-based methodologies for analyzing cultural
  narratives and stories

  – Step-by-step guides for revealing hidden cultural as-
  sumptions and frameworks

  – Practical techniques for identifying key cultural concepts
  in everyday speech

- Powerful approaches to uncovering identity dynamics through storytelling

- Ready-to-use exercises to practice cultural analysis methods

Step 3: Develop Equal Alternative Narratives

Step 3 sits at the heart of the process. This is where we translate our understanding from Steps 1 and 2 into actionable strategies. By knowing **how** the IBD manipulates needs and narrows identity (Step 1) and **who** our target audience is, **what they value**, and **what needs are important to them** (Step 2), we can craft resonant alternatives. In this step, we'll identify positive values to amplify and develop "equal alternative narratives" that fulfill the same underlying needs as the IBD, but in non-divisive, healthy, and inclusive ways.

As in the previous steps, use the included worksheet and AI prompts at the end of this guide to assist you and refer to the next chapter's real world case study implementation example, which is particularly valuable as a reference for this critical step.

Part 3A: Identify Positive Values & Alternative Need Fulfillment

This part focuses on bridging the gap between understanding the problem (IBD tactics and audience needs) and creating the solution (positive alternatives).

1. How to Infer Positive Values to Emphasize:

Instead of just listing examples, let's think about *how* to find the right positive values. Review your findings from Steps 1 & 2 and ask:

- **What's the Opposite?** What positive value is the direct opposite of the IBD's negative framing or the narrow identity it promotes? (e.g., If IBD promotes *exclusion* to create belonging, the opposite value is *inclusion* or *community*).

- **What's Being Undermined?** What positive values (like fairness, empathy, critical thinking) does the IBD actively try to suppress or discredit in the target audience? These are often ripe for reinforcement.

- **What's Being Distorted?** Does the IBD twist a value the audience genuinely holds dear (e.g., patriotism, tradition, faith)? Identify the *authentic, positive, and inclusive* version of that value held by the community.

- **What Does the Audience Already Value (Step 2)?** Look at the core values, identity layers, and aspirations you identified in your target audience analysis (Step 2). Which of these offer a constructive counterpoint to the IBD's narrative? Which resonate most strongly?

- **What Universal Values Apply?** What fundamental human values (like kindness, respect, cooperation, seeking truth) align with the audience's culture and directly counter the IBD's divisiveness?

2. How to Generate Alternative Ways to Fulfill Needs:

The IBD offers a harmful shortcut to meet genuine needs. Our goal is to brainstorm *healthy, constructive, and culturally resonant* alternatives. For each need the IBD exploits (identified in Step 1), ask:

- **What Already Exists (Step 2)?** What positive community activities, traditions, support systems, or social groups *already* exist within the target audience's culture (identified in Step 2) that genuinely meet this need? (e.g., If IBD offers belonging through an online hate group, what *local clubs, volunteer groups, family traditions, or faith communities* offer healthy belonging?)

- **How Can Aspirations Be Channeled (Step 2)?** What hopes, goals, or aspirations identified in Step 2 can be linked to fulfilling this need positively? (e.g., If IBD offers significance through aggression, how can the audience's aspiration for *community improvement* provide significance?)

- **What Cultural Resources Can Be Used (Step 2 & later in Step 3)?** What stories, symbols, historical examples, or respected figures from the audience's culture offer inspiring ways to meet this need? (e.g., Stories of past community resilience to meet the need for security).

- **How Can We Offer *Multiple* Options?** The IBD often presents only one narrow path. Brainstorm *several diverse and inclusive* ways the audience can meet the need, reflecting the complexity of real life. (e.g., Self-esteem can come from work, family, hobbies, learning, helping others, etc., not just the single source the IBD promotes).

3. Apply this Thinking using the Framework:

Now, use the insights above to fill out the framework. For each underlying need:

- **Underlying Need:** (e.g., Belonging and Love)

  - **How the IBD Exploits This Need:** [Summarize your analysis from Steps 1 & 2, focusing on the specific tactics and the audience's vulnerability]

  - **Inferred Positive Values to Emphasize:** [List the values you identified using the prompts in 3A.1 above, e.g., Community, inclusion, shared heritage, family bonds, mutual respect]

  - **Generated Alternative Ways to Fulfill This Need:** [List the concrete, positive strategies you brainstormed using the prompts in 3A.2 above, e.g., Highlight inclusive community traditions, celebrate diverse expressions of belonging, showcase stories of intergenerational connection, promote participation in local groups]

- **Underlying Need:** (e.g., Self-Esteem, Status & Significance)

  - **How the IBD Exploits This Need:** [Your analysis from Steps 1 & 2]

  - **Inferred Positive Values to Emphasize:** [e.g., Achievement, contribution, cultural pride, personal growth, integrity, diverse talents]

  - **Generated Alternative Ways to Fulfill This Need:** [e.g., Showcase diverse success stories (not just one type), emphasize multiple paths to respect, celebrate contributions to family/community, highlight skills development opportunities]

- **Underlying Need:** (e.g., Equality & Justice)

  - **How the IBD Exploits This Need:** [Your analysis from Steps 1 & 2]

  - **Inferred Positive Values to Emphasize:** [e.g., Fairness, mutual respect, cooperation, dialogue, due process, empathy]

  - **Generated Alternative Ways to Fulfill This Need:** [e.g., Share stories of justice achieved through collaboration, highlight historical examples of positive social change, promote constructive dialogue methods, emphasize shared community standards]

- **Underlying Need:** (e.g., Freedom from Fear and Suffering (Security))

  - **How the IBD Exploits This Need:** [Your analysis from Steps 1 & 2]

  - **Inferred Positive Values to Emphasize:** [e.g., Resilience, adaptability, mutual protection, shared strength, preparedness, community safety initiatives]

  - **Generated Alternative Ways to Fulfill This Need:** [e.g., Emphasize historical examples of overcoming challenges *together*, showcase community support systems, promote practical safety/preparedness skills, highlight stories of collective problem-solving]

Part 3B: Develop Equal Alternative Narrative Strategies

Now that you have identified positive values and alternative ways to meet needs, you need to strategize *how* to weave these into narratives that resonate without triggering backlash.

Important: Your goal is NOT to directly counter the IBD message. Your goal is to **expand the target audience's identity options**, making them less susceptible to the narrow identity frames offered by IBD.

Based on the positive values and alternative need fulfillments identified above, brainstorm specific narrative approaches:

- **Focus on Identity Expansion:** How can your narratives provide multiple ways for the target audience to express their values and fulfill their needs? (e.g., Showcasing different types of community contribution, highlighting diverse expressions of faith or tradition).

- **Avoid Direct Reference to the "Other":** Ensure your narratives focus solely on the target audience's positive identity and community, never mentioning or implicitly referencing the group targeted by the IBD.

- **Circumvent Triggering Backlash:** Frame narratives positively and constructively. How can you present these ideas as natural extensions of the audience's existing values, rather than direct challenges to the IBD? (e.g., Frame inclusivity as strengthening community bonds, rather than as a rebuttal to exclusionary IBD).

- **Meet Needs Authentically:** How can the narratives genuinely satisfy the needs identified, using culturally resonant stories and examples? Ensure the fulfillment offered feels real and achievable within the audience's context.

Strategy Considerations (Examples):

- **For "Us-Them" IBD Narratives:** Focus on broadening the concept of "us" by celebrating *internal diversity* within the target audience's own community or culture. Highlight shared goals or values that cut across potential dividing lines *within* the group.

- **For Fear-Based IBD Narratives:** Instead of directly challenging fears, provide concrete stories of *local resilience*, community cooperation in overcoming past challenges, or practical steps individuals can take to enhance *shared security*.

- **For Status/Pride IBD Narratives:** Showcase *multiple, diverse avenues* for members of the target audience to gain respect, feel pride, and achieve significance (e.g., through skill mastery, community service, artistic expression, family dedication) beyond the narrow path offered by the IBD.

Part 3C: Find Cultural References

Authentic cultural references are key to making your narratives resonate. Research confirms that authentic, culturally resonant references are highly effective (see Chapter 10: Academic Research Supporting the Toolkit for details).

Look for examples from the target audience's culture (drawing on your Step 2 analysis) that support your equal alternative narratives. This could include:

- **Famous Figures:** Historical or contemporary figures known for embodying complexity, resilience, or inclusive values relevant to the audience.

- **Literary Works/Oral Traditions:** Books, poems, songs, or widely known stories that celebrate cooperation, adaptability, or diverse expressions of identity.

- **Proverbs or Idioms:** Local sayings that reflect wisdom about navigating complexity, community strength, or inclusive values.

- **Historical Events:** Specific local or national events that demonstrate successful cooperation, adaptation, or overcoming division.

- **Cultural Practices/Symbols:** Traditions, rituals, or symbols that represent shared positive values like community, resilience, or mutual support.

Choose references that are:

- **Deeply Resonant:** Genuinely meaningful to the target audience.

- **Largely Uncontroversial:** Avoid references likely to be highly divisive *within* the target audience.

- **Supportive of Expansion:** Align with the goal of broadening identity options.

Pro Tip: Before heavily relying on a cultural reference (like a historical figure or proverb), subtly test its resonance. Does it come up naturally in conversations? Is it viewed positively by diverse segments of your audience? A reference that seems perfect on paper might carry unintended baggage.

Part 3D: Create Your Narrative Framework

Now, consolidate your work from Parts 3A, 3B, and 3C into a structured framework. Use the **Narrative Development Worksheet** (provided at the back of this guide) or create your own document based on this structure for each key need/value pair:

- **Underlying Need Targeted by IBD:** (e.g., Security)

- **How IBD Exploits It:** [Your analysis]

- **Inferred Positive Value(s) to Emphasize:** (e.g., Resilience, Community Cooperation)

- **Generated Alternative Need Fulfillment Strategy:** (e.g., Showcase stories of past community resilience, promote participation in neighborhood watch)

- **Specific Narrative Angle/Strategy:** (e.g., Focus on shared strength in overcoming challenges, emphasize practical community safety measures)

- **Potential Cultural References:** (e.g., Local historical event of overcoming adversity, proverb about unity, respected elder known for resilience)

This framework will serve as your detailed roadmap for crafting specific messages in Step 5, ensuring they are strategically grounded in your analysis and designed to expand identity options effectively.

Use the AI prompt for narrative creation (referenced at the back of the guide) for guided assistance. See how the case study achieves this step by reading the next chapter of this guide.

Action Point: When developing strategies and finding references, constantly ask: "How does this connect to the *specific* cultural and historical context of *this* audience?" Avoid generic approaches; root your narratives in their lived reality, ideally validated through consultation or dialogue with members of the audience to ensure authenticity and resonance.

Step 4: Identify Trusted Voices and Channels

Having developed potential narrative strategies in Step 3, the focus now shifts to *how* these narratives will reach the target audience effectively. Even the most carefully crafted alternative narrative will fail if it isn't delivered by a credible source (a trusted voice) through a platform the audience actually uses and pays attention to (an appropriate channel). This step is crucial because trust is the gateway for any message to be considered, especially in environments saturated with disinformation. Identifying the right voices and channels

ensures your narratives have the best chance of being heard and resonating authentically.

Trusted Voices:

Who does the target audience genuinely trust and listen to? Consider individuals and groups who hold credibility *within the specific
context* you are working in. This might include:

- Local leaders (mayors, community organizers, respected
  elders)

- Religious figures (priests, imams, rabbis, pastors relevant to
  the audience)

- Family members and close friends (often the most influential)

- Teachers and educators

- Local celebrities or micro-influencers genuinely respected by
  the community (use with caution)

- Specific media personalities or journalists known for fairness
  or local focus

Communication Channels:

Where does the target audience get their information and spend
their time? Effective channels are those the audience already uses
and trusts. Consider:

- Social media platforms (Which specific ones? Facebook
  groups, Instagram, TikTok, Twitter/X, WhatsApp group chats?)

- Local newspapers, community websites, or blogs

- Community newsletters or bulletins

- Local radio or television stations

- Places of worship (sermons, study groups, notice boards)

- Community centers, libraries, local shops, pubs, or cafes

- Word of mouth within existing social networks

Write it Down: Based on your Step 2 audience analysis and further research, list the most promising trusted voices and communication channels for your specific target audience. Document *why* you believe they are trusted or relevant.

Pro Tip: Don't just assume someone is trusted based on their role. Verify it. Observe who the audience naturally listens to, shares content from, and engages with positively. Sometimes the most influential voices aren't the most obvious ones (e.g., a local shop owner, a specific grandparent, a popular coach might be more trusted on certain community matters than a distant politician or generic celebrity).

Identifying these key voices and channels prepares you for Step 5, where you will tailor the specific messages for delivery through these pathways. Use the AI prompt for identifying trusted voices and channels (referenced at the back of the guide) for assistance.

Step 5: Craft Your Equal Alternative Narratives

With your strategic narrative framework developed (Step 3) and your trusted voices and channels identified (Step 4), this step focuses on translating that preparation into specific, actionable content. Now it's time to craft the actual messages—the stories, posts, images, or videos—that will carry your alternative narratives to the target audience through the pathways you've chosen. Research supports strategic approaches to content delivery, such as sequencing messages and using culturally authentic elements (see Chapter 10: Academic Research Supporting the Toolkit).

Message Creation Framework

- **Content Strategy Foundations**

  - Apply Positive Identity Expansion Principles: Create messages that fulfill the same psychological needs as the IBD but through positive, inclusive means.

  - Lead with Value Fulfillment: Focus first on meeting the fundamental needs you identified in Step 3A (belonging, self-esteem, security, justice).

  - Embed Multiple Identity Pathways: Showcase various ways people can express the same values or fulfill the same needs, reinforcing the identity expansion goal from Step 3B.

  - Cultural Authenticity: Root your content in genuine cultural expressions and references identified in Step 3C that resonate deeply with the target audience.

- **Practical Message Crafting Guidelines**

  - Voice and Tone

    * Match Authentic Community Language: Study how respected voices (identified in Step 4) in the community naturally communicate—use similar vocabulary, sentence structures, and expressions.

    * Cultural Resonance: Incorporate cultural touch-points (from Step 3C) that signal insider understanding.

    * Emotional Calibration: Aim for emotional resonance that feels natural rather than manipulative.

    * Avoid Activism Markers: Carefully eliminate language patterns that might signal your content as part of a "campaign" or "initiative."

  - Content Structure

    * Storytelling Formula: Where possible, use the classic narrative structure of context → challenge → resolution → meaning.

    * Multiple Entry Points: Design content that appeals to different segments within your target audience (identified in Step 2).

    * Clarity with Nuance: Communicate clearly while preserving the natural complexity of identity and

values.

* Platform-Specific Optimization: Adapt your message format to the conventions of each channel identified in Step 4 (thread structure for Twitter, carousel posts for Instagram, etc.).

- Strategic Emphasis

  * Need Fulfillment First: Clearly address the fundamental needs the IBD exploits (identified in Step 3A), but in healthier ways.

  * Value Amplification: Highlight the positive values inferred in Step 3A that counter the IBD's narrow identity offerings.

  * Identity Expansion: Show multiple ways to express identity while maintaining core values, aligning with strategies from Step 3B.

  * Subtle Critical Thinking: Encourage reflection without directly challenging beliefs.

- **Message Development Process**

  1. **Draft Basic Message Framework (Using Step 3D Framework):** For each key need/value combination outlined in your narrative framework (created in Step 3D), draft the core components of your message:

     - Core message (1-2 sentences capturing the essence)

- Supporting narrative elements (key points, story arc ideas)

- Potential visual components (image ideas, video concepts)

- Key emotional response you hope to evoke (positive, connecting)

2. **Cultural Enhancement (Using Step 3C References):** Weave in the specific cultural references identified in Step 3C to make the message authentic and resonant:

   - Incorporate relevant figures, stories, proverbs, events, or practices.

   - Use language or symbols that align with the audience's cultural context.

3. **Platform Adaptation (Using Step 4 Channels):** Customize your drafted content for the specific communication channels identified in Step 4:

   - Twitter/X: Concise, engaging hooks with strategic hashtags.

   - Instagram: Visually compelling, authentic imagery with carefully crafted captions.

   - Facebook: More detailed storytelling with community engagement elements.

 – TikTok/Short Video: Authentic, relatable moments that feel spontaneous rather than scripted.

 – Community Forums: Conversation starters that invite genuine dialogue.

- **Message Examples with Strategic Rationale** *(Illustrating strategies like celebrating internal diversity, highlighting local resilience, showcasing multiple paths to success)*

Consider approaches like the "Hook, Line, Sinker" method for sequencing content (detailed further in the chapter Best Practices for Deployment). The following examples illustrate how to apply the framework:

 – Example Set 1: Fulfilling Belonging & Love Needs *(Strategy: Highlighting intergenerational connection & inclusive tradition)*

   * Image Message: [Community members of various ages working on a traditional craft project]

   * Caption: "When Grandma Chen taught me how to make these lanterns, she said, 'Our hands remember what our ancestors knew.' Now I'm teaching my daughter—and her friends want to learn too! What traditions are you passing down? #HeritageKeepers #OurTraditions"

   * Strategic Rationale:
     · Need Addressed: Belonging through intergenerational connection

- Values Emphasized: Tradition, community, knowledge sharing

- Identity Expansion: Shows tradition as inclusive rather than exclusive

- Cultural Authenticity: References specific cultural practice (lantern making)

- Example Set 2: Fulfilling Self-Esteem & Significance Needs *(Strategy: Redefining strength through adaptability & continuity)*

  * Video Content: Brief interview with a community elder sharing wisdom

  * Caption: "Mr. Jackson has lived in our town for 87 years. He's seen changes that would amaze you. 'The strong ones,' he says, 'are those who know both where they come from AND where they're going.' Who are the wisdom-keepers in your community? #RespectOurElders #WisdomKeepers"

  * Strategic Rationale:
    - Need Addressed: Significance through connection to heritage and future

    - Values Emphasized: Respect for elders, adaptability, strength in continuity

    - Identity Expansion: Redefines strength to

include both tradition and change

- Cultural Authenticity: Centers community elder as wisdom source

- Example Set 3: Fulfilling Security Needs *(Strategy: Emphasizing community solidarity & resilience)*
    * Image: Historical photo of community recovering from past hardship alongside contemporary community cooperation

    * Caption: "Our town has faced challenges before. In 1953, when the floods came, neighbors helped neighbors rebuild. Today, we face different challenges, but that spirit of looking out for each other remains our greatest strength. #CommunityResilience #TogetherWeEndure"

    * Strategic Rationale:
        - Need Addressed: Security through community solidarity

        - Values Emphasized: Resilience, mutual support, historical continuity

        - Identity Expansion: Shows how community values persist through changing times

        - Cultural Authenticity: References specific historical event meaningful to the community

- Example Set 4: Fulfilling Justice & Equality Needs *(Strategy: Recognizing diverse contributions to community strength)*

  * Image Series: Community members of different backgrounds contributing to local projects

  * Caption: "In our town, everyone has something valuable to contribute. From Coach Rivera organizing youth sports to Ms. Kim leading the community garden—it's the different skills and perspectives that make our community thrive. What's your unique contribution? #CommunityStrengths #EveryoneMatters"

  * Strategic Rationale:

    · Need Addressed: Equality through recognition of diverse contributions

    · Values Emphasized: Fairness, mutual respect, recognition

    · Identity Expansion: Shows how different roles and backgrounds strengthen community

    · Cultural Authenticity: Names real local figures (use actual community members)

- **Message Documentation Template** *(Use the Narrative Development Worksheet or a similar template)*

For each message you create, document:

- Message ID: [Number/Code]

- Need Addressed: [Primary need this fulfills]

- Values Emphasized: [List 2-3 key values]

- Identity Expansion Strategy: [How it broadens identity options]

- Target Platform: [Where this will be shared]

- Content Type: [Image/Video/Text/Poll/etc.]

- Caption/Text: [Full text]

- Visual Elements: [Description of images/video]

- Hashtags: [List relevant tags]

- Cultural References: [Specific cultural elements incorporated]

- Expected Engagement: [How you anticipate audience will respond]

- Risk Assessment: [Potential for misinterpretation or co-option]

Use the AI prompt for message crafting (referenced at the back of the guide) for guided assistance.

Pro Tip: Start small. Before launching a full suite of messages, test a few key narratives with a small, trusted subset of your target audience or advisors. See what resonates, what falls flat, and what might be misinterpreted. Iterate based on this initial feedback.

Having crafted these specific messages, the next step (Step 6) involves considering the strategic design and subtlety required for effective deployment.

Step 6: Strategic Narrative Design

Now that you have crafted potential messages in Step 5, Step 6 focuses on the crucial strategic considerations for their deployment. Effective alternative narratives often require subtlety to avoid triggering defensive reactions or being dismissed as 'counter-messaging'. Your goal is to design how your narratives are presented so they act as authentic cultural celebration or common-sense observations, allowing them to resonate more deeply. Adapting narratives to the specific local context is crucial for effectiveness, an approach supported by research (see chapter: Academic Research Supporting the Toolkit).

Approach Principles

- Use Collaborative Consultation/Dialogical processes to Incorporate Narratives Indigenous to the Culture: Ensure narratives emerge organically from the target audience's existing cultural ecosystem through active participation and dialogue. This principle is best achieved through genuine co-creation or deep consultation *with* members of the target audience, allowing their "ordinary ways" and perspectives to shape the narrative. The goal is for narratives to extend natural expressions of the community's values, not form as externally imposed messages.

- Focus on Celebration, Not Opposition: Frame your narratives as celebrations of the target community's values, achievements, and traditions—not as responses to anything negative.

- Use Established Cultural Channels: Distribute your messages through existing, trusted community channels rather than creating obviously new "counter-disinformation" platforms.

- Embrace Complexity and Nuance: Include appropriate complexity that reflects real cultural expressions. Overly simplified or perfect narratives may appear suspicious or contrived.

Strategic Invisibility Assessment

For each equal alternative narrative you've developed, conduct this assessment:

- Visibility Analysis

  - Is it obviously a counter-narrative? Check whether your message appears to be directly responding to specific IBD claims.

  - Does it use oppositional language? Look for terms like "actually," "despite what you may have heard," or "the truth is" that signal opposition.

- Would it attract negative attention? Consider whether the narrative might trigger defensive reactions from those spreading IBD.

- Refinement Techniques

  - Cultural Embedding: Root your narratives deeply in existing cultural traditions, celebrations, or historical references that already resonate with the target audience.

  - Positive Framing: Ensure your messages are framed entirely in positive terms rather than as corrections to something negative.

  - Narrative Distance: Create appropriate distance between your narrative and the topics of the IBD by focusing on related but distinct aspects of the target audience's identity.

  - Temporal Shifting: Connect your narratives to historical traditions or future aspirations rather than current controversies.

Example Refinements

Original Approach (Too Obvious)	Refined Approach (More Subtle)
"Unlike what some say about our community, we've always welcomed different perspectives."	"Our community's strength has always come from our ability to listen to different viewpoints and find common ground."
"Don't believe the myths about our religious traditions—they've always been compatible with modern values."	"Exploring how our religious traditions have adapted through generations while maintaining their core wisdom."
"The idea that we must choose between tradition and progress is false."	"Celebrating the ways our community has carried forward cherished traditions while embracing new opportunities."

Practical Exercise: The Invisibility Test

For each narrative you develop, apply the "invisibility test" by asking:

- Would an IBD agent recognize this as opposition? If yes, refine it.

- Does it directly reference or contradict specific IBD talking points? If yes, shift focus to affirmative values rather than corrections.

- Can this narrative stand on its own merit? It should be compelling and meaningful even if the IBD didn't exist.

- Would it be shared naturally by community members? The narrative should feel authentic enough that people would share it organically.

- Does it expand identity options without appearing to do so deliberately? The expansion of identity options should emerge naturally from the stories and examples shared.

The most effective alternative narratives operate below the radar of IBD agents while simultaneously fulfilling the same needs the IBD exploits, but in healthier, more inclusive ways. By making your narratives as authentic cultural expressions rather than counter-strategies, you increase their effectiveness and reduce the risk of triggering backlash or adaptation by IBD agents.

What If They Notice? Managing IBD Agent Reactions

Despite your best efforts to create subtle alternative narratives, IBD agents may notice your activity and attempt to co-opt, discredit, or use your messages as fuel for their campaigns. When this happens, strategic response is crucial.

When IBD Agents Target Your Narratives

- Assess the Situation Before Responding:

  - Is the IBD agent's attack gaining traction within your target audience?

  - Has the core message of your alternative narrative been significantly distorted?

  - Are community members expressing confusion or concern?

- Strategic Non-Engagement:

  - In most cases, direct confrontation or defense of your narrative will only amplify the IBD agent's message and draw more attention to their claims.

  - Remember that engaging directly can validate their framing and position them as an equal "side" in a debate.

  - Strategic silence often deprives IBD messaging of the oxygen of attention it requires to spread.

- Consider Framing and Association: Be mindful of how your response might unintentionally reinforce the IBD agent's framing. Sociological research on framing highlights that how a message is presented matters significantly. Right-wing propagandists often normalize harmful ideas by associating familiar words in new ways (e.g., "teachers" and "grooming"). When countering or proposing alternatives, consider using different vocabulary if the IBD agent has already heavily loaded a particular term with negative connotations. Directly engaging with their chosen terms, even to debunk them, can sometimes inadvertently strengthen the association they seek to create.

Factors to Consider in Your Decision:

Consider Disengaging When:	Consider Continued Engagement When:
The IBD agent's response has minimal reach	Vulnerable community members are being specifically targeted
Your alternative narrative continues to spread positively elsewhere	Significant confusion about core values is occurring
Direct engagement would elevate the IBD message	You can provide support without directly addressing the IBD
The attack is primarily aimed at you personally rather than the message	The benefits of clarification clearly outweigh the risks

If You Choose to Continue Engagement

When you determine that continued engagement would benefit your target audience:

- Redirect Rather Than Defend:

    - Instead of directly defending against attacks, redirect attention to positive examples and stories.

    - Use phrases like "What's really important here is…" to refocus on your core values.

- Amplify Community Voices:

- Rather than speaking yourself, amplify the voices of respected community members who naturally embody the values you're promoting.

- This provides "social proof" without appearing defensive.

- Create New Narratives:

  - Sometimes the best response is to create entirely new alternative narratives that fulfill the same needs but are distinct enough to avoid the IBD agent's focus.

  - These new narratives should maintain continuity with your values while approaching from a fresh angle.

- Support Targeted Community Members:

  - Provide private support and resources to community members who may feel confused or targeted by the IBD response.

  - This behind-the-scenes work often has more impact than public engagement.

Long-term Resilience Building

Whether you choose to engage or not, focus on building long-term resilience:

- Diversify Your Approaches:

- Don't rely on a single narrative or communication channel.

- Develop multiple, complementary alternative narratives that support each other.

- Build Support Networks:

    - Connect with others doing similar work to share experiences and strategies.

    - Create mutual support systems for when challenges arise.

- Document Patterns:

    - Keep track of IBD agent tactics and responses to inform future approaches.

    - This documentation can help identify evolving strategies and prepare better responses.

Remember that your ultimate goal is expanding identity options for your target audience, not winning arguments with IBD agents. Every decision about engagement should be guided by what best serves this core purpose, balancing risks and benefits carefully based on the specific context and potential impact on your community.

Pro Tip: Regularly apply the "invisibility test" from this section to your drafted messages. Ask yourself honestly: "Could this be easily mistaken for a direct attack or rebuttal?" If so, revise it to focus more on positive celebration and shared values. True subtlety is key.

By carefully considering these strategic design elements and planning how to manage potential reactions, you increase the likelihood
that your alternative narratives will be received positively and contribute effectively to identity expansion. The final step before deployment (Step 7) involves a thorough review and refinement process.

Step 7: Review, Refine, and Share Responsibly

Before sharing your equal alternative narratives, conduct a comprehensive review to ensure they're effective, authentic, and ethically
sound. This final quality control step is crucial for maximizing positive impact while minimizing potential risks.

Comprehensive Review Checklist

- **Content Quality**

    - Accuracy: Is all information factually correct and verifi-
      able?

    - Authenticity: Does it genuinely resonate with the target
      audience's values and lived experiences?

    - Cultural Relevance: Are cultural references appropriate
      and meaningful to the audience?

    - Narrative Depth: Does the content have sufficient depth
      to be engaging while remaining accessible?

- **Strategic Effectiveness**

- Need Fulfillment: Does it address the same underlying needs that the IBD exploits, but in a healthy, constructive way?

- Strategic Subtlety: Would it appear as an authentic cultural expression rather than an obvious counter-strategy?

- Identity Expansion: Does it actively expand the target audience's identity options rather than narrowing them?

- Multiple Pathways: Does it present diverse ways to express values rather than a single "correct" approach?

- **Risk Assessment**

  - No "Other" Mentions: Confirm there are no explicit references to the group targeted by the IBD.

  - Potential for Misinterpretation: Consider how the message might be misunderstood or twisted.

  - Unintended Implications: Check for potentially problematic subtext or implications.

  - Cultural Sensitivities: Ensure the content respects cultural nuances and avoids inadvertent offense.

- **Structural Elements**

  - Clarity and Accessibility: Is the message clear, concise,

and easily understood by the target audience?

- Linguistic Appropriateness: Does the language match how the target audience naturally communicates?

- Emotional Resonance: Does it connect emotionally without manipulating emotions?

- Visual Harmony: If using images, do they align with and enhance the message?

Feedback and Refinement

- **Gather Diverse Feedback from the Target Audience:**

  - Community Representatives: Share draft content with trusted members of the target audience who understand their community's nuances and can provide an "emic" perspective. This might include individuals within your own network if they belong to or are close to the target audience.

  - Cultural Advisors: Consult with individuals who have deep knowledge of the cultural context.

  - Initial Testing: Where feasible, test how draft messages land with a small, representative group from the target audience. Are the narratives understood as intended? Do they resonate authentically? Do they inadvertently trigger negative reactions?

- **Create a Structured Feedback Process:** Develop specific questions to guide feedback, focusing on resonance, clarity, potential misinterpretations, and alignment with the audience's lived reality.

- **Refinement Guidelines**
  - Iterative Improvement: Be prepared to go through multiple revisions.

  - Balance Feedback: Consider all input but prioritize perspectives from those closest to the target audience.

  - Maintain Core Purpose: Ensure refinements don't dilute the fundamental aim of expanding identity options.

  - Test Against Objectives: After each revision, check that the content still fulfills the needs identified in your analysis.

Responsible Sharing

- **Strategic Dissemination**
  - Timing Considerations: Choose optimal timing that aligns with natural community rhythms and relevant events.

  - Channel Appropriateness: Share through the trusted channels identified in Step 4, ensuring format matches platform expectations.

  - Authentic Voice: If possible, have respected community members share the content rather than positioning yourself as an outside voice.

- Natural Integration: Introduce narratives in ways that feel organic to existing conversations rather than abruptly changing topics.

Monitoring and Learning

- Establish a systematic approach to track impact:

    - Engagement Metrics: Monitor quantitative measures like shares, comments, and reach.

    - Qualitative Analysis: Assess the nature and tone of responses, particularly looking for signs of expanded identity expression.

    - Network Effects: Track how the narrative spreads and evolves as community members adapt and share it.

    - Emergence Indicators: Look for signs that community members are spontaneously creating similar content that expands identity options.

    - Adaptive Management: Be prepared to make real-time adjustments based on how your narratives are received and shared.

Documentation and Learning

- Maintain a Reflection Journal: Document what works, what doesn't, and surprising outcomes.

- Create a Learning Repository: Build a knowledge base of effective approaches for your specific context.

- Share Insights Responsibly: Consider how your lessons learned might help others, while protecting sensitive information.

- Practice Self-Care: Monitor your own well-being during this process, as countering IBD can be emotionally demanding.

Remember that effective equal alternative narratives evolve organically and authentically within communities. Your role is to thoughtfully introduce and nurture these narratives, then allow the community to adapt and own them. Success often looks like your narratives spreading naturally, with your direct involvement becoming increasingly unnecessary as the community embraces expanded identity options.

Pro Tip: Don't skip the feedback step! Getting diverse perspectives on your drafted messages *before* sharing widely is crucial for catching potential misinterpretations, cultural blind spots, or unintended consequences. It's better to refine based on feedback than to cause accidental harm.

7 Implementation Case Study: Applying the 7 Steps

Having outlined the 7 key steps for implementing the Reclaiming Our Narrative toolkit in the previous chapter, let's now see how these steps apply in practice. We will use the **"Trojan Horse" Hoax in UK Schools (Example 4 from the chapter Historical and Contemporary Examples of IBD)** as a detailed case study to illustrate the application of each step in a real-world scenario.

Scenario Recap: A fake letter alleging an "Islamist plot" to take over schools in Birmingham, UK, was leaked to the media. This caused a moral panic, damaged the careers of Muslim educators, and strained community relations, despite the letter being a fabrication.

Our Goal (Applying the Toolkit): To walk through each of the 7 implementation steps, demonstrating how to analyze the hoax (Step 1), define the target audience (Step 2), develop equal alternative narratives (Step 3), identify channels (Step 4), craft messages (Step 5), ensure subtlety (Step 6), and review responsibly (Step 7). As with all Positive Identity Expansion applications, the ultimate aim is to build resilience within the *target audience* (the concerned non-Muslim public) against the fear and suspicion generated by the hoax, using narratives that expand identity options without directly confronting the hoax itself.

Step 1: Analyze the IBD Campaign (The "Trojan Horse" Hoax)

1. **Gather Examples:**

    - The fake "Trojan Horse" letter itself.

    - Sensationalist media headlines ("Islamist plot," "radicals replacing teachers").

    - Social media posts expressing fear/outrage.

    - Public statements from politicians demanding action.

    - Ofsted's emergency inspections and reports (even if later nuanced, the initial action fueled the narrative).

    - Anecdotes of suspicion towards Muslim staff/governors.

2. **Identify Themes:**

    - Secret, hostile takeover of institutions by an internal "enemy."

    - Threat to children's safety and innocence (indoctrination).

    - Undermining of "British values."

- Muslim community members (especially educators/governors) are inherently suspect.

- Existing systems (schools, local councils) are failing to protect against this threat.

3. **Identify Emotions:**

- **Fear:** For children's safety, cultural integrity, national security.

- **Suspicion/Distrust:** Towards Muslim neighbours, colleagues, officials.

- **Anger/Indignation:** At the alleged plotters and perceived institutional failures.

- **Resentment:** Potential existing anxieties about multiculturalism or Islam channeled into this specific issue.

- **Moral Panic:** A widespread feeling of exaggerated threat.

4. **Needs Analysis:**

- **Security (Freedom from Fear):** Directly exploited by framing Muslims in schools as a physical and ideological threat to children and British society. The hoax promised security through vigilance and exclusion.

- **Belonging:** Manipulated by creating an "us" (concerned Britons protecting values) versus "them" (secretive

Muslim plotters). Belonging was made conditional on sharing suspicion. Exploited by framing the alleged plot as an attack on the continuity of British values and way of life within schools.

- **Self-Esteem/Significance:** Offered a sense of virtue or significance to those "speaking out" or demanding action against the perceived threat.

- **Equality/Justice:** Twisted – the narrative framed the (non-existent) plot as unjust, thereby justifying potentially unjust actions (suspensions, negative inspections) against the accused. Offered a false sense of 'doing justice' by "doing something" by demanding investigations, firings, or stricter controls, based on fear rather than facts.

5. **Identify Identity Manipulation:**

- **Narrowed "British Identity":** Promoted a version where being "truly British" meant being suspicious of Muslim civic participation and prioritizing a narrow definition of "British values" over principles like fairness or due process in this context.

- **Narrowed "Muslim Identity":** Portrayed engaged Muslim citizens (teachers, governors) not as assets but as potential threats, making their civic identity suspect.

6. **Identify False Choices:**

- "You must choose between trusting Muslim educators/-

governors OR protecting children and British values."

- "You must choose between supporting multicultural integration OR ensuring school safety and security."

- "You must choose between believing the official processes OR believing the 'evidence' of the plot (the letter/rumors)."

7. **Analyze Power Dynamics:**

- **Power Holders:** Significant power was wielded by national media outlets (amplifying the hoax), government figures (like the Education Secretary reacting strongly), and Ofsted (whose investigations lent official weight). The anonymous letter author held initial disruptive power. Conversely, the accused Muslim educators and governors possessed far less institutional power to counter the narrative.

- **Resource Disparities:** Media and state actors had vast resources for dissemination and investigation, dwarfing the capacity of the targeted individuals and schools to respond effectively.

- **Influence on Narrative:** The hoax gained traction partly because it tapped into existing societal anxieties and stereotypes. The authority of media headlines and official investigations made the narrative seem more credible, overriding the lack of concrete evidence for the "plot."

- **Impact on Reach and Reception:** The narrative spread widely through established, powerful channels (national press, government pronouncements). The target audience likely gave weight to these official/media sources, making it difficult for counter-arguments from the less powerful accused group to gain equal hearing or trust.

8. **Write it Down (Summary):** The Trojan Horse hoax used a fake document, amplified by media and official reactions, to create a moral panic. It exploited fears for child safety and cultural continuity, framing Muslim educators as a hidden threat. It offered security and belonging through suspicion, creating a false choice between inclusion and safety, thus narrowing both British and Muslim identities within the public sphere.

Step 2: Define and Understand Your Target Audience

Crucial Distinction: Our target audience is **NOT** the British Muslim community being attacked. It is the **wider non-Muslim public in Birmingham and the UK** who were exposed to the hoax and potentially influenced by it – parents, other educators, media consumers, policymakers.

1. **Comprehensive Audience Analysis:**

- **Demographics:** Broad, but particularly parents with children in Birmingham schools, residents of affected areas, consumers of specific media outlets (tabloids, certain mainstream news), potentially individuals with pre-existing anxieties about Islam or immigration.

- **Identity Ecosystem:** Strong identities likely include: British national identity, local Birmingham pride, parental identity (protective), professional identity (for educators), potentially religious identity (Christian), political affiliations. Possible tension: valuing fairness vs. prioritizing safety based on alarming reports.

- **Psychological Profile:** Core Values: Child safety, education quality, fairness, community cohesion, rule of law, "British values" (potentially varied interpretations). Needs: **Security** (paramount regarding protecting children), **Belonging** (local community, national 'British Values'). Pain Points: Fear of extremism/terrorism, anxiety about social change, feeling that institutions aren't responsive. Aspirations: Safe and effective schools, harmonious community life.

- **Information Landscape:** Trusted Sources: School communications, Ofsted reports (seen as authoritative), local council, mainstream media (BBC, Guardian, but also tabloids like Mail, Sun), social media (local parent groups, community pages), word-of-mouth within school/community networks.

2. **Research Methods (Hypothetical):** Monitor local Birmingham Facebook parent groups, analyze coverage across different UK newspapers, review official statements from Ofsted/Council/Govt, perhaps conduct (if feasible) informal

conversations with parents/residents *not* directly involved to gauge general sentiment.

3. **Audience Archetype:** "Concerned Birmingham Parent": Mid-30s to 50s, values children's safety above all, gets news from local media and BBC/ITV, active on school WhatsApp/Facebook group, respects Ofsted, feels anxious when hearing about extremism, wants to trust schools but easily alarmed by official-sounding warnings or scary headlines. *Variations:* National media consumer, local politician, non-Muslim teacher in Birmingham.

4. **Vulnerability Assessment:** Highly vulnerable to narratives triggering **fear** related to child safety. Susceptible to appeals to "common sense" vigilance that bypass due process. May trust official investigations (Ofsted) even if the premise (the hoax) is flawed. Prone to believing negative stories if they fit pre-existing anxieties.

Step 3: Develop Equal Alternative Narratives

This step translates the analysis from Steps 1 & 2 into concrete narrative strategies for the Trojan Horse scenario. Knowing the IBD exploited fears around **Security (Child Safety, Protecting Children/Community)** and **Belonging (Shared Community, British Values)**, and targeted the **Concerned Beirmingham Parent's** need for **Security** and **Belonging**, we can now develop alternatives.

Part 3A: Identify Positive Values & Alternative Need Fulfillment (Trojan Horse Context)

Applying the guidance from the main Step 3:

1. Inferring Positive Values:

- **Opposite of IBD:** The hoax promoted *suspicion* and *panic*; the opposite values are *trust (in process)*, *calm*, and *evidence-based assessment*.   It created *division*; the opposite is *community cohesion* and *shared goals*.

- **Values Undermined:** The hoax undermined *fairness*, *due process*, *professional respect* for educators, and *trust in institutions*. These need reinforcement.

- **Values Distorted:** The hoax distorted "British values" into something exclusionary.   The authentic, inclusive version emphasizes *fair play*, *tolerance*, and *rule of law*.

- **Audience Values (Step 2):** The "Concerned Parent" values *child safety*, *education quality*, *fairness*, and *community*. We can leverage these existing values.

- **Universal Values:** *Respect*, *cooperation*, and *seeking truth* counter the hoax's divisiveness.

2. Generating Alternative Need Fulfillments:

- **Need: Security (Child Safety, Protecting Children/Community):**

  - *Existing Resources:* Highlight established, rigorous school safeguarding policies, teacher vetting (DBS checks), and Ofsted's standard inspection framework (contrasting it with the emergency reaction). Promote official channels for raising school concerns (talking to headteachers, governors, Ofsted via standard procedures). Highlight constructive roles like PTA involvement or volunteering.

- *Aspirations:* Channel parental desire for safety into constructive engagement like understanding existing safety protocols or participating in school governance properly. Channel desire to "do something" into promoting media literacy or supporting evidence-based discussions.

- *Cultural Resources:* Emphasize the professionalism and dedication expected of UK educators. Appeal to the value of responsible citizenship and supporting due process.

- *Multiple Options:* Security comes from robust systems, professional staff, *and* calm, evidence-based community vigilance through official channels, not panic. 'Doing something' to protect and seek justice means engaging constructively through established systems, not demanding action based on rumour.

- **Need: Belonging (Shared Community, British Values):**

  - *Existing Resources:* Focus on existing cross-community initiatives in Birmingham (interfaith groups, shared civic projects), shared identity as parents wanting good schools, local/regional cultural pride. Frame *fairness, tolerance, rule of law, and evidence-based judgment* as core British values being upheld.

- *Aspirations:* Channel desire for community into celebrating *shared goals* for education and the city's success. Channel desire to protect British values into actively demonstrating fairness and resisting prejudice.

- *Cultural Resources:* Use Birmingham's history of diverse communities working together. Reference the principle of "fair play," historical examples of British justice and tolerance.

- *Multiple Options:* Belonging comes from shared civic identity, neighbourhood connections, common goals – not from uniting against a perceived internal enemy. Upholding British values means ensuring fairness and due process for all, not succumbing to panic.

3. Applying to the Framework (Summary):

- **Need: Security (Child Safety, Protecting Children/-Community).** *IBD Exploited:* Fear of extremist teachers. Panic-driven demands for action. *Inferred Positive Values:* Professionalism, effective safeguarding, evidence-based action. Responsible citizenship, critical thinking, supporting due process, constructive engagement. *Generated Alternative Fulfillment:* Highlight robustness of existing school safety measures, celebrate dedication of *all* staff, promote official channels for concerns. Narratives emphasizing constructive ways parents *can* support schools (volunteering, PTA), promoting media literacy, reinforcing trust in established procedures.

- **Need: Belonging (Shared Community, British Values).** *IBD Exploited:* Us vs. Them based on religion/culture. Threat of "Islamization." *Inferred Positive Values:* Shared civic identity, common goals (good education), diverse contributions, community cohesion. Fairness, justice, tolerance, evidence-based decision-making (as core British values). *Generated Alternative Fulfillment:* Stories about successful cross-community projects *in Birmingham*, highlighting shared parental goals, celebrating diversity as a strength. Narratives explicitly linking "British values" to fairness, due process, and rejecting prejudice; historical examples of the UK overcoming division.

Part 3B: Develop Equal Alternative Narrative Strategies (Trojan Horse Context)

Based on the above, we strategize *how* to present these alternatives:

- **Focus on Identity Expansion:** Provide narratives where the "Concerned Parent" can see themselves as being *both* vigilant about safety *and* fair-minded; proud of British values *including* tolerance and due process; part of a strong community *because* of its collaborative spirit across differences.

- **Avoid Direct Reference to the "Other":** Do not mention "Muslims," "Islam," or the specifics of the hoax letter. Focus entirely on positive actions and values within the broader school/Birmingham community context.

- **Circumvent Triggering Backlash:** Frame narratives around universal concerns (child safety, school quality) and established positive norms (professionalism, fair process).

Presenting information about existing safeguarding feels like helpful reassurance, not a rebuttal. Celebrating community cohesion feels like civic pride, not a defence.

- **Meet Needs Authentically:** Offer genuine reassurance through highlighting real systems (safeguarding). Provide concrete, constructive actions for active seeking out of justice and problem solving (using official channels). Ground belonging in shared civic identity and goals.

Strategy Considerations (Examples):

- **Countering "Us-Them":** Focus on the *internal diversity and shared goals* of Birmingham parents and educators. Frame narratives around "all our children," "our dedicated school staff," "our city's strength."

- **Countering Fear:** Provide concrete information about *existing safety protocols* and the *professionalism* of vetted staff. Share stories of *calm, evidence-based responses* to challenges.

- **Countering Status/Pride (of being vigilant):** Reframe pride around *upholding fairness* and *supporting due process* as demonstrations of strength and true British values.

Part 3C: Find Cultural References (Trojan Horse Context)

Drawing from Step 2 and the above:

- **Famous Figures:** Possibly quotes from respected British legal figures on justice, or educators on professionalism (used generically).

- **Literary/Oral Traditions:** The concept of "fair play" in British culture.

- **Proverbs/Idioms:** Sayings about "keeping calm," "looking before you leap," or community strength.

- **Historical Events:** Birmingham's history of rebuilding community post-WWII or navigating industrial change through cooperation. Examples of the UK justice system upholding fairness in difficult times.

- **Cultural Practices/Symbols:** The established procedures of Ofsted inspections (standard vs. emergency), the formal process for school governance, the professional codes of conduct for teachers.

Part 3D: Create Your Narrative Framework (Trojan Horse Example Snippet)

- **Underlying Need Targeted by IBD:** Security (Child Safety)

- **How IBD Exploits It:** Fear of extremist infiltration in schools.

- **Inferred Positive Value(s) to Emphasize:** Professionalism, effective safeguarding, evidence-based action, calm assessment.

- **Generated Alternative Need Fulfillment Strategy:** Highlight robustness of existing school safety measures (vetting, policies), celebrate dedication of *all* staff, promote official channels for raising concerns constructively.

- **Specific Narrative Angle/Strategy:** Focus on reassurance through competence and process. Frame vigilance as using established procedures correctly, not succumbing to rumour.

- **Potential Cultural References:** UK teacher vetting standards (DBS checks), Ofsted's standard inspection framework, the principle of "innocent until proven guilty" applied to processes, the value placed on professional qualifications in the UK.

Step 4: Identify Trusted Voices and Channels

To ensure the alternative narratives developed in Step 3 reach the target audience effectively, we must identify credible messengers and appropriate platforms, drawing on the audience analysis from Step 2.

For the Target Audience (Concerned Public):

1. **Trusted Voices:**

    - Respected Headteachers (especially those seen as neutral, experienced, perhaps from schools *not* directly targeted but in the same area).

    - Local Council officials responsible for education (if perceived as competent and non-political on this).

- Representatives from established teaching unions or governor associations (speaking about processes).

- Leaders of interfaith groups in Birmingham.

- Possibly moderate journalists or local bloggers known for balanced reporting.

- *Less likely:* Politicians heavily involved in the controversy, or groups explicitly defending the accused (seen as biased by the target audience).

2. **Communication Channels:**

   - Local Media: Birmingham Mail, BBC Midlands Today, local radio.

   - School Communication: Newsletters, school websites, official parent communication platforms.

   - Community Hubs: Libraries, community centers (posters, leaflets).

   - Online: Council websites, trusted local Facebook groups (parenting, community news), potentially local forums like Mumsnet Birmingham.

   - National Media: Broadsheet newspapers (Times, Guardian) for more nuanced takes, potentially BBC News.

Step 5: Craft Your Equal Alternative Narratives (Messages)

Now, we translate the narrative framework (Step 3) into specific messages tailored for the trusted voices and channels identified (Step 4).

Applying Hook, Line, Sinker & Cultural References:

- **Example Set 1: Focusing on Process & Professionalism (Need: Security, Agency)**

    - **Hook (Image on Local News Site/Social Media):** Stock photo of diverse teachers collaborating. Caption: "Did you know? All UK school staff undergo rigorous checks. Our teachers are dedicated professionals committed to every child's success." #SupportingOurSchools #ProfessionalEducators

    - **Line (Article/Blog by Headteacher Union Rep):** "Keeping Our Schools Safe: Understanding Safeguarding Procedures." Explains the established, robust processes schools use daily, emphasizing evidence and professional judgment. (Uses trusted voice, focuses on system strength).

    - **Sinker (School Newsletter/Council Website):** "Have a concern about your child's school? There are clear, established ways to raise issues constructively with school leadership and governors. Let's work together through the right channels." (Promotes action for justice/protection through legitimate means).

- **Example Set 2: Focusing on Community Cohesion (Need:**

Belonging, Security)

- **Hook (Photo Series on Community FB Group):** Pictures from a recent successful, diverse Birmingham community event (unrelated to schools). Caption: "Birmingham shines when we all pull together! Great turnout at the [Event Name] this weekend." #BrumSpirit #CommunityPride (Celebrates positive shared identity).

- **Line (Local Radio Interview):** Feature on a long-running interfaith project in Birmingham, highlighting cooperation and shared goals. (Uses local reference, shows positive interaction).

- **Sinker (Flyer at Community Centre):** "Building a Stronger Birmingham: We all want the best for our children and our city. Let's focus on what unites us – shared goals for education, safety, and community." (Appeals to shared values).

- **Example Set 3: Focusing on Fairness as a Value (Need: Belonging, Justice)**

  - **Hook (Quote Graphic on Social Media):** "Fairness and judging on evidence – core British values we teach our children. Let's apply them ourselves." #FairPlay #BritishValues (Uses cultural reference).

  - **Line (Op-Ed in Local Paper by Interfaith Leader):** "In challenging times, our city's strength lies in upholding justice and resisting division based on rumor." (Connects fairness to resilience).

- **Sinker (Discussion Prompt in Online Forum):** "How can we ensure our community discussions about important issues remain respectful and fact-based, even when concerns are raised?" (Encourages reflection on process).

Documentation: Each message would be logged using the template (ID, Need, Values, Platform, Text, etc.).

Step 6: Strategic Narrative Design

1. **Subtlety Principles:**

   - Frame messages positively around existing strengths (professionalism, safeguarding, community spirit, fairness).

   - Avoid mentioning "Trojan Horse," "hoax," "Islamist plot," or directly defending Muslim staff.

   - Use channels natural for discussing education and community matters (school newsletters, local news features on education).

   - Appear as routine positive messaging about good school practice and community values.

2. **Invisibility Assessment:**

- **Test:** Does "Highlighting robust safeguarding procedures" look like a direct counter? No, it looks like standard good practice communication.

- **Test:** Does "Celebrating Birmingham's diverse community events" look like a rebuttal? No, it looks like standard community pride.

- **Refinement:** An initial idea like "Don't judge all Muslim governors by a fake letter" is too direct. Refine to: "Let's appreciate the hard work of *all* volunteer governors dedicated to our schools." (Subtly inclusive, positive framing).

3. **Managing Reactions:** If someone comments on a post about "safeguarding procedures" with "But what about the Trojan Horse plot?", the strategy is **not to engage** on the hoax. Instead:

   - **Redirect:** "Thank you for your concern for school safety. The established procedures we've highlighted are designed to address any genuine issues effectively through proper channels." (Re-emphasizes the positive alternative framework).

   - **Amplify:** Share a comment from another parent saying, "Good to know these procedures are in place."

   - **Ignore/Moderate:** If comments become abusive or fixated on the hoax, ignore or moderate based on platform rules, without debating the IBD narrative.

Step 7: Review, Refine, and Share Responsibly

1. **Comprehensive Review Checklist:**

   - **Accuracy:** Are the descriptions of safeguarding proce-
     dures correct? Yes.

   - **Authenticity:** Does the language sound like it's from
     school leaders or community groups? Yes.

   - **Cultural Relevance:** Does "fair play" resonate? Yes. Are
     local references accurate? Yes.

   - **Strategic Effectiveness:** Does it fulfill needs (security,
     belonging) positively? Yes. Does it expand identity (fair,
     evidence-based citizen)? Yes.

   - **Risk Assessment:** Could "celebrating diversity" be
     attacked as "PC nonsense"? Possibly, but the risk is
     lower than directly confronting the hoax. Ensure focus
     remains on shared goals. No 'Othering' is present.

2. **Feedback and Refinement (Hypothetical):** Share draft messages with a diverse group of Birmingham parents and educators (who weren't targets of the hoax investigations) for a
   reality check. Ask: "How does this message make you feel?"
   "Is anything unclear or potentially offensive?" "Does it sound
   genuine?" Refine based on feedback (e.g., adjust tone, clarify
   jargon).

---

3. **Responsible Sharing:**

  - Use the identified channels (school newsletters, local news education sections, council web pages, trusted community groups).

  - Have trusted voices (headteachers, union reps, interfaith leaders) deliver or endorse the messages where possible.

  - Introduce narratives gradually, integrating them into existing communications about school quality, community events, or civic values.

4. **Monitoring and Learning:**

  - Track engagement on social media posts (likes, shares, *tone* of comments).

  - Listen for shifts in conversation in parent groups – less panic, more focus on process or positive school aspects.

  - Note if media coverage starts incorporating more nuanced language around school governance or community relations.

  - Observe if people start organically sharing similar positive messages. Adapt based on what resonates.

Conclusion of Case Study:

By following these steps, a practitioner could develop and deploy equal alternative narratives targeting the concerned public during the Trojan Horse affair. Instead of, or in addition to, directly debunking the hoax, the focus would be on reinforcing positive values like fairness, evidence-based safety, and community cooperation. These narratives aim to fulfill the audience's legitimate need for security and belonging in constructive ways, expanding their identity options beyond the narrow, fear-based reactions promoted by the IBD. This builds long-term resilience by making the audience less susceptible to future divisive manipulation targeting the same underlying needs and anxieties.

8 Ethical Guidelines for Narrative Development

Ethical Guidelines and Responsible Use

This toolkit empowers you to take action against identity-based disinformation (IBD), but with that power comes responsibility. The goal is to build bridges, not walls; to strengthen communities, not further divide them. This section provides both general ethical guidelines and a structured framework to help you make sound decisions in challenging situations.

General Ethical Guidelines

1. **Do No Harm**: Your primary goal should be to promote positive values and strengthen communities. Avoid any actions that could cause harm or exacerbate existing tensions.

2. **Respect Diversity**: Recognize and celebrate the diversity of experiences and perspectives within the target audience. Avoid generalizations and stereotypes.

3. **Promote Critical Thinking**: Encourage people to think critically about all information, including the content you create.

Don't try to manipulate or deceive anyone, even with good intentions.

4. **Be Transparent**: Be open about your intentions and your use of this toolkit. Don't misrepresent yourself or your motives.

5. **Protect Privacy**: Be mindful of privacy concerns when gathering and sharing information. Don't share personal information without consent.

6. **Prioritize Accuracy**: Ensure that all information presented is factually correct and verifiable. Take great care not to spread misinformation, even unintentionally.

7. **Avoid Reinforcement**: Do not repeat or amplify the IBD narratives, even when attempting to counter them. Focus only on the positive alternatives.

8. **Focus on the Positive**: Always frame your messages in a positive and constructive way. Avoid negativity, attacks, and ANY "us vs. them" rhetoric.

9. **Take this Seriously**: IBD is a serious threat, and countering it requires careful consideration and responsible action.

10. **Seek Further Training**: If you are considering practicing countering IBD more professionally, consider seeking formal training. See the Related Organizations and Initiatives chapter.

11. **Avoid Validation and Manipulation**: Never validate the factual claims or harmful premises of IBD narratives, even implicitly while addressing underlying needs.

12. **Seek to Empower:** Ensure your strategies genuinely empower the audience through Positive Identity Expansion,

rather than subtly manipulate them towards an alternative narrative - the target audience must *want* to choose the alternative.

Navigating Cultural Authenticity Ethically

While Step 6 emphasizes using authentic cultural celebration to make narratives resonate, this principle must operate within strict ethical boundaries. Cultural authenticity or tradition can **never** justify actions or narratives that cause harm, incite hatred, promote discrimination, or violate fundamental human dignity.

- **Universal Ethics Prevail:** Appeals to cultural identity are subordinate to universal ethical principles like "Do No Harm," respect, fairness, and truthfulness.

- **Reject Harmful Traditions:** Be critical of cultural elements that inherently promote exclusion, violence, or dehuman-ization. Not all traditions are ethically neutral or positive. History tragically shows that horrific ideologies and actions (like Nazism or other genocidal regimes) have sometimes been cloaked in appeals to distorted notions of cultural purity or destiny. Such justifications are fundamentally unethical.

- **Focus on Positive & Inclusive Aspects:** When drawing on culture, focus on traditions, stories, and values that promote inclusivity, empathy, cooperation, and resilience in ethically sound and universally human ways.

- **Context is Key, but Not an Excuse:** Understanding cultural context is vital for effectiveness, but it cannot excuse the promotion of harmful ideas. The goal is to find *positive* and *ethical* ways to meet needs within a cultural context, not to use culture as a shield for harmful narratives.

Ethical Decision-Making Framework: The R.E.S.P.E.C.T. Model

When faced with a difficult ethical dilemma, use this framework to guide your decision-making:

R - Recognize the Ethical Issue

- Is there a conflict of values?

- Does something feel "wrong" or uncomfortable?

- Could this action potentially cause harm?

- Does this situation go beyond a simple question of right and wrong?

E - Explore the Facts and Context

- What are the relevant facts of the situation?

- Who are the stakeholders involved (who will be affected)?

- What are the potential consequences of different actions?

- What are the underlying needs and motivations of the target audience?

- What are the specific IBD narratives at play?

- What are the cultural norms and sensitivities of the target audience?

S - Seek Multiple Perspectives

- Talk to trusted friends, family members, or community members

- Consider the perspectives of people from different backgrounds and viewpoints

- Consult with experts or organizations working on countering disinformation

- Ask yourself: "How would someone I respect approach this situation?"

P - Principles and Values

- What are the core ethical principles at stake (e.g., honesty, respect, fairness, responsibility, compassion)?

- Which values are most important in this situation?

- Are there any conflicting principles? If so, how can you prioritize them?

- How do the general ethical guidelines of this toolkit apply?

E - Evaluate Potential Actions

- List the possible courses of action

- For each action, consider:

  - What are the potential benefits?

  - What are the potential risks and harms?

  - Who will be affected, and how?

  - Does this action align with the ethical principles and values you've identified?

  - Does this action align with the goals of positive identity expansion and building resilience?

  - Could this action be misinterpreted or misused?

C - Choose and Act

- Based on your evaluation, choose the course of action that best aligns with your ethical principles and values

- Be prepared to explain and justify your decision

- Act with courage and conviction, but also with humility and a willingness to learn

T - Track, Reflect, and Learn

- Monitor the consequences of your actions

- Reflect on the outcome: Did your action have the intended effect?

- Learn from your experience and adjust your approach as needed

Example Application of the R.E.S.P.E.C.T. Model

Scenario: You're creating a social media post to promote community unity. You're considering using a humorous meme that pokes fun at a stereotype, but you're worried it might be offensive to some people.

- **Recognize**: There's a potential conflict between humor and respect for diversity

- **Explore**: The stereotype targets a specific subgroup within the community

- **Seek**: Ask friends from different backgrounds for their opinions

- **Principles**: Respect for diversity, avoiding harm, and promoting inclusivity are key

- **Evaluate**:

    - Option 1: Use the meme (risky)

    - Option 2: Don't use the meme (safe)

    - Option 3: Modify the meme (still risky)

    - Option 4: Create a different message (recommended)

- **Choose**: Create a different message that promotes unity without stereotypes

- **Track**: Monitor response and reflect on effectiveness

9 Best Practices for Deployment

Research supports the importance of strategic content delivery for maximum impact of Positive Identity Expansion strategies. There is great value in creating layered, interconnected content. In this chapter, we introduce some deployment models and best practices to help you get going with an interconnected content ecosystem that unfolds strategically over time.

Strategic Sequencing and Content Ecosystems

Narrative Arc Approaches

The Hook, Line, and Sinker Method

Here is an example of a helpful implementation method:

"Hook: Share historical photos of community celebrations with caption: 'Our town's heritage festivals have always brought people together. What's your favorite memory from past celebrations?' "

"Line: Post about a respected community elder: 'Meet Ms. Johnson, who has organized our heritage festival for 30 years. She believes the festival's strength comes from how it evolves while honoring traditions.' "

"Sinker: 'Our community's story is written by all of us, in different ways but with shared pride. How would you like to contribute to this year's heritage celebration?'"

This approach includes:

- **Hook**: Begin with visually striking, emotionally resonant content that captures attention

- **Line**: Follow with deeper context that reinforces positive identity values

- **Sinker**: Introduce content addressing underlying needs with multiple healthy pathways

Value Immersion Cycles

- Dedicate 1-2 weeks exploring different facets of specific positive values

- Rotate through varied perspectives addressing common needs

- Create natural transitions between value cycles

Narrative Weaving Strategy

- Develop 3-5 complementary narrative threads

- Alternate between threads to maintain engagement

- Create "callback" moments referencing earlier content

Effective Question Framing

- Use "what" and "how" questions instead of "why" questions

- Provide example responses to model desired tone

- Example questions:

    - "What tradition in our community makes you most proud?"

    - "How has our community supported you during challenging times?"

    - "Share a memory of when you felt our shared values in action"

Visual Content Guidelines

Research supports the importance of culturally authentic visual content.

Guidelines:

- Use authentic imagery reflecting community diversity

- Prioritize emotional resonance over technical perfection

- Include culturally specific visual elements (research shows these generate the highest trust and engagement)

- Maintain consistent visual themes and styles

- Create shareable community templates

Community Engagement Strategies

Research on overcoming prejudices demonstrates the effectiveness of deliberative citizen dialogues that allow participants to engage with multiple perspectives.

Research-backed engagement strategies:

- **Micro-Engagement**: Personalize responses to small interactions

- **Amplification**: Elevate positive community contributions

- **Cross-Pollination**: Connect similar interests

- **Bridge-Building**: Link different perspectives

- **Conversation Stewardship**: Guide toward constructive exchanges

Monitoring and Adaptation

Success Indicators

- Track quantitative metrics (engagement, sharing, growth)

- Monitor qualitative changes (conversation tone, identity expressions)

- Observe behavioral shifts in community expression

Feedback Integration

- Collect diverse feedback channels

- Focus on patterns over outliers

- Align adjustments with core objectives

- Test changes with small groups first

Improvement Cycle

- Establish regular review periods

- Document successes and challenges

- Build effective approaches repository

- Reassess needs periodically

Safety Framework

Personal Security

- Conduct risk assessments

- Use dedicated profiles

- Set clear boundaries

- Create accountability partnerships

Emotional Resilience

- Set engagement time limits

- Develop self-care routines

- Monitor for burnout

- Build support networks

Community Protection

- Develop clear guidelines

- Create moderation plans

- Establish escalation procedures

- Prepare support resources

Nuancing the Role of Facts

The primary strategy of this toolkit focuses on positive identity expansion rather than direct fact-checking or debunking. However, this doesn't mean facts are irrelevant! There may be specific, limited circumstances where carefully introducing factual elements or prompting critical thinking about sources can be considered.

When Might Factual Elements Be Considered?

- **After Establishing Identity Options and Trust:** Once alternative narratives are in circulation and trust and use of these has been demonstrated, the audience *might* be more receptive to gentle questioning or subtle factual corrections.

- **Focusing on Source Credibility:** Instead of directly refuting a claim, you might prompt reflection on the source of the IBD. E.g., "Where did this information originally come from?" or "What might be the motivations of the group sharing this?"

- **Highlighting Internal Contradictions:** Gently pointing out inconsistencies *within* the IBD narrative itself, rather than contrasting it with external facts, can sometimes encourage critical thinking without triggering defensiveness.

- **Providing Alternative Factual Narratives:** Instead of debunking a negative claim, offer a positive, factual narrative that implicitly counters it. E.g., instead of "Claim X about

Group Y is false," share a true, positive story about Group Y's contributions that fulfills similar needs (like security or community pride).

Key Cautions:

- **Avoid Direct Confrontation:** Never frame factual information as a direct attack on the audience's beliefs.

- **Prioritize Needs:** Ensure any factual element still serves the primary goal of fulfilling underlying needs positively.

- **Context is Crucial:** The appropriateness depends heavily on the specific audience, the nature of the IBD, and the relationships you've built and options have have/don't have to express their needs.

- **High Risk:** Introducing factual corrections remains risky and can easily undo progress if not handled with extreme sensitivity.

- **Focus on Questions:** Often, posing open-ended questions ("What evidence supports this view?", "Are there other ways to look at this?") is safer and more effective than asserting facts directly.

In summary, while positive identity expansion is the core strategy, a nuanced understanding allows for the possibility of carefully integrating fact-based elements or critical thinking prompts in specific, later-stage contexts, always prioritizing the relationship and the audience's underlying needs over simply being "right."

Emphasizing Cultural and Contextual Depth

As highlighted throughout the implementation steps, truly effective alternative narratives must be deeply rooted in the specific cultural, historical, traditional, and even mythological context of the target audience. Generic messages often fall flat because they lack the resonance and authenticity that come from genuine cultural understanding.

Why Deep Context Matters:

- **Authenticity and Trust:** Narratives that incorporate specific local proverbs, historical anecdotes, respected figures, or traditional stories feel more authentic and are more likely to be trusted. They signal "insider" understanding.

- **Addressing Underlying Worldviews:** IBD often taps into deep-seated cultural anxieties or beliefs. Effective alternatives must engage with this same level of cultural depth, offering positive interpretations or pathways rooted in the audience's own heritage.

- **Resonance:** Culturally specific references evoke stronger emotional responses and create more memorable connections than generic statements. Research shows the power of culturally embedded narratives.

- **Avoiding Misinterpretation:** A lack of deep contextual understanding can lead to messages being misinterpreted or even causing unintended offense. What seems like a positive symbol in one context might have negative connotations in another.

Best Practices for Ensuring Depth:

- **Go Beyond Surface Symbols:** Don't just use obvious flags or holidays. Explore deeper cultural narratives, foundational myths, influential artistic traditions, core religious tenets (as understood locally), and pivotal historical moments that shape identity.

- **Engage Cultural Advisors:** Collaborate with trusted individuals who possess deep, nuanced knowledge of the target audience's culture and history. Listen actively to their insights and feedback.

- **Prioritize Lived Experience:** Ground your narratives in the real-life experiences and perspectives of the community. Use language, examples, and storytelling styles that feel natural and familiar to them.

  - **Understand Local Interpretations:** Recognize that cultural symbols or historical events can be interpreted differently even within the same broad culture. Understand the *local* meaning and significance.

  - **Apply in the Field:** This toolkit is designed to be applied *in context*. The analysis and narrative development should happen with continuous reference to the specific environment and audience, not in a vacuum.

  - **Uphold Ethical Boundaries:** Crucially, the pursuit of cultural depth must always be guided by the ethical principles outlined in the previous chapter. Authenticity cannot be used to justify or excuse narratives that promote harm, hatred, or violate universal human dignity.

By prioritizing deep cultural and contextual understanding **within clear ethical boundaries**, your alternative narratives move from being simply "messages" to becoming meaningful contributions to the community's own story, making them far more powerful in building resilience against IBD.

10 Academic Research Supporting the Toolkit

Research Foundation

The "Reclaiming Our Narrative" toolkit is grounded in evidence-based approaches to understanding and countering identity-based disinformation (IBD). Key research findings have been incorporated throughout the toolkit to ensure that the strategies and methods recommended are supported by academic evidence. This chapter highlights key studies and research principles that inform the toolkit's approach.

The approach draws particularly on established interdisciplinary insights on how identity functions from **psychological anthropology** (understanding identity's layered and symbolic nature, including the concept of multiple, context-dependent identity positions; Gregg, 1991, 1998; Quinn, 2006), **narrative psychology** (how stories shape identity; Hammack, 2008, 2010), and **neurobiology** (mechanisms of memory formation and change; LeDoux, 2002; Ecker & Vaz, 2022). For more on the key interdisciplinary theoretical models and works used in understanding how identity forms and functions, the reader might consult some of the works in the extended bibliography below, and/or refer to articles hosted at the OICD website (oicd.net).

Key Research Studies

Beyond foundational theory, the practical approach contained in this guide is also informed by a rich body of academic literature. While drawing on the expertise of its creators and the broader field of counter-disinformation research referenced below, the following studies are particularly highlighted throughout the toolkit:

1. **Taiwan Election Study (Bhattacharya et al., 2024)**

   - Analyzed how symbolic content impacts user engagement and trust on TikTok during Taiwan's 2024 election

   - Found that cultural symbols generated the highest engagement and trust levels, emerging as *"the most potent trust-builders, garnering a trust percentage of about 62%."* They were also found to be *"powerful catalysts for positive sentiment, eliciting the highest proportion of joy and the lowest levels of negative emotions."*

   - Demonstrated a synergistic effect when combining multiple symbol types (social, cultural, political), with the highest engagement observed when all three were present: *"The continued increase in engagement through Categories 2 and 3 suggests a synergistic effect when multiple symbol types are combined, with the highest engagement observed when all three symbol types (social, cultural, and political) are present."*

2. **Overcoming Prejudices Study (Yabanci, 2024)**

- Examined how deliberative citizen dialogues affected attitudes toward refugees in Turkey

- Found that de-stigmatizing narratives (e.g., drawing on *"the collective memory of forced migration proved to be a compelling narrative for fostering a sense of fairness and moral obligation towards refugees."*) evoked empathy and led to more moderate attitudes

- Demonstrated the effectiveness of narrative sharing over argumentative approaches

- Highlighted the importance of local context, finding that positive attitudes displayed *"a local turn, varying by city,"* noting: *"Local dynamics play an essential role in shaping citizens' attitudes towards refugees. Factors such as ethnic identity and historical background of residents in each city influenced how people perceived and responded to presented narratives."*

3. **OPPATTUNE Methods Handbook (Rottmann et al., 2025)**

- Highlighted the limitations of direct confrontation with extremist narratives (which often backfires) and the effectiveness of alternative approaches

- Outlined effective methods for **narrative dialogue groups** as a constructive alternative, emphasizing that such approaches should be *"dynamic, flexible and contextually-based"*

Research-Supported Principles

The academic literature validates the toolkit's core principles, which are grouped here thematically:

Theme 1: The Effectiveness of Positive Identity Expansion

Positive Identity Expansion vs. Direct Confrontation

- Research confirms that directly challenging deeply held beliefs often leads to defensiveness and a resistance to change, especially when core identity beliefs are involved (Bar-Tal, 2020). Attempts to debunk can even strengthen the targeted belief (the "backfire effect"). IBD often creates "semantic barriers"—using language to dismiss alternative views (Gillespie, 2020b).
- Studies show narrative-based approaches are often more effective than direct arguments. Positive Identity Expansion, drawing on narrative psychology and the concept of identity flexibility, aims to foster **psychological adaptability** and restore **identity agency** (the sense of control over one's identity). It does this by offering appealing alternative narratives that meet underlying needs without triggering defensiveness.
- *(This principle underpins the entire toolkit's strategy, particularly* **Step 3: Develop Equal Alternative Narratives***, by explaining why offering positive options is often more effective than direct debunking.)*

Meeting Underlying Needs

- Evidence demonstrates that addressing fundamental human needs (belonging, self-esteem, security, meaning) in healthy, constructive ways is crucial for well-being and resilience (e.g., Frankl, 2010). IBD often exploits unmet needs by offering harmful, narrow solutions (Sen, 2008).

- Research shows that building trust and relationships is essential for effective dialogue aimed at shifting perspectives (Yabanci, 2024). Focusing on shared needs and values helps build this trust.

- *(This directly informs **Step 1: Analyze the IBD Campaign** and **Step 3A: Identify Positive Values & Alternative Need Fulfillment**, guiding the focus towards addressing the audience's genuine needs constructively.)*

Theme 2: Understanding Psychological Mechanisms and Vulnerability

Psychological Flexibility and Optionality

- Positive Identity Expansion promotes **narrative optionality**—giving people more choices in how they understand themselves and their world (Sen, 2008; Splitter, 2020). This counteracts the narrowing effect of IBD.

- It engages the **symbolic and emotional dimensions of identity** (Gregg, 1991; Hammack, 2008), offering appealing alternatives (juxtapositions) that fulfill needs constructively.

- This approach aims to update deeply held, unhelpful narratives by providing compelling alternative identity pathways, leveraging **memory reconsolidation** (Ecker & Vaz, 2022) processes to maximize the opportunity for the alternative to be employed.

- It contrasts with mechanisms often exploited by IBD, such as

motivational imbalance (where one need, like significance, overrides others, leading to extremism; Kruglanski et al., 2021) and **moral disengagement** (justifying harmful actions by selectively ignoring broader values; Bandura, 2002, 2015).

- By fostering identity flexibility and providing multiple healthy ways to meet needs and express values ("optionality of needs" and "optionality of moral values"), this approach aims to make individuals less susceptible to manipulation.
- *(Understanding these mechanisms helps refine the strategies in **Step 3** and **Step 5**, ensuring narratives promote psychological flexibility.)*

The Fusion-Plus-Threat Model

- Research highlights the danger when **identity fusion** (an intense merging of personal and group identity) combines with a **perceived existential threat** to that group (Whitehouse, 2018; Ebner et al., 2022). This combination strongly predicts willingness to engage in extreme actions, often more so than ideology alone.
- Linguistic analysis of extremist manifestos shows that markers of fusion (e.g., kinship language like "brothers") and threat perception are prevalent in violent texts but rare in non-violent ones (Ebner et al., 2022).
- IBD tactics often seek to induce states similar to fusion (promoting intense, narrow group loyalty) while simultaneously manufacturing a sense of threat (e.g., "they are destroying our way of life").
- *(This model further highlights the risks IBD poses and reinforces the importance of the toolkit's approach in **Steps 1, 3, and 5** to avoid creating conditions conducive to harmful fusion and per-*

*ceived threat. **Positive Identity Expansion aims to prevent and reverse fusion by promoting multiple identity facets and mitigate threat perceptions by offering constructive ways to address needs like security.**)*

Message Framing and Word Associations

- Research on message framing shows that *how* something is said is crucial. Propagandists often normalize harmful ideas by associating familiar words in new, negative ways (Scatton, 2025).
- It's important to deliberately create positive associations and avoid repeating or directly negating negative frames, as even negation can reinforce the unwanted concept (Lakoff, 2004; 2008; Scatton, 2025).
- *(This research directly informs **Step 5: Craft Your Equal Alternative Narratives** and **Step 6: Strategic Narrative Design**, emphasizing careful language choice and the creation of new, positive reference points.)*

Heightened Vulnerability and Ontological Security

- Vulnerability to IBD often increases during times of significant societal change or personal trauma. These experiences can create profound uncertainty or **ontological insecurity**—a disruption to one's stable sense of reality and trust (Giddens, 1991; Kinnvall, 2004; Rottmann et al., 2025).
- When ontological security is threatened, individuals may be more drawn to narratives that offer simple explanations, clear enemies, and a promise of restored stability, even if these narratives are divisive or based on falsehoods (Andreouli et al., 2024; Kinnvall, 2004). IBD often exploits this by scapegoating

specific groups for societal problems.

- *(Recognizing ontological insecurity informs the sensitivity required in **Step 2: Define and Understand Your Target Audience** and the need to provide reassuring, constructive narratives in **Step 5** that address underlying anxieties about security and belonging without resorting to harmful 'us vs. them' framing.)*

Theme 3: The Power of Culture and Context

Cultural References and Symbols

- Studies confirm that cultural symbols are powerful catalysts for positive sentiment and trust (Bhattacharya et al., 2024). Narratives using culturally specific elements resonate more deeply.
- Research shows culturally relevant narratives are particularly effective at changing attitudes (Yabanci, 2024).
- Culture often plays a more significant role than explicit ideology in group commitment, shaping perceptions and even allowing for contradictory beliefs (Andreouli et al., 2024; Blee, 2007; McClusky, 2019). Understanding the target audience's cultural framework is therefore essential.
- *(This research strongly supports **Step 3C: Find Cultural References** and **Step 5: Craft Your Equal Alternative Narratives**, emphasizing the need for culturally authentic content.)*

Local Context Adaptation

- Studies emphasize that effective interventions must be tailored to specific communities and be "dynamic, flexible and contextually-based" (Rottmann et al., 2025, p. 63). Generic approaches are less likely to succeed.

- Research shows that local dynamics (history, demographics, social tensions) significantly influence how narratives are received and interpreted (Yabanci, 2024; Rottmann et al., 2025).
- *(This principle is crucial for **Step 2: Define and Understand Your Target Audience** and **Step 6: Strategic Narrative Design**, highlighting the need to tailor narratives to specific local realities.)*

Theme 4: Strategic Delivery and Impact

Strategic Content Delivery

- Evidence supports the effectiveness of sequencing content delivery (like the Hook, Line, Sinker method mentioned in Chapter 9).
- Research validates combining different types of symbols (social, cultural, political) for synergistic impact (Bhattacharya et al., 2024).
- *(This informs **Step 5: Craft Your Equal Alternative Narratives** and **Step 6: Strategic Narrative Design**, particularly regarding sequencing and combining different message elements.)*

Individual Action Building Community Resilience

- Evidence suggests that micro-level interventions (individual actions, local initiatives) can contribute to broader social change and build community resilience.
- Research confirms that strengthening everyday social bonds and community connections is vital for resilience against divisive forces (cf. Atran, 2011).

- *(This principle provides the rationale for the toolkit's empowerment of individuals, as outlined in **Chapter 2: The Power of Individual Action**.)*

References

Andreouli, E., Ghosh, S., Ricarte, J., Rottmann, S., Weilnböck, H., & Leitão, A. (2024). *D5.1 Framework paper on emergence of opposition drivers across sites and shared dialogical interventions*. OPPATTUNE Project.

Atran, S. (2011). *Talking to the Enemy: Violent Extremism, Sacred Values, and What It Means to Be Human*. Penguin Books.

Bandura, A. (2002). Selective moral disengagement in the exercise of moral agency. *Journal of Moral Education*, 31(2), 101–119.

Bandura, A. (2015). *Moral disengagement: How people do harm and live with themselves*. New York: Worth Publishers.

Bar-Tal, D. (2020). Conflict-supporting narratives and the struggle over them. In A. Mana & A. Srour (Eds.), *Israeli and Palestinian narratives in conflict: A tribute to Shifra Sagy and her work* (pp. 36-60). Cambridge Scholar Publishers.

Bhattacharya, S., Agarwal, N., & Poudel, D. (2024). Analyzing the impact of symbols in Taiwan's election-related anti-disinformation campaign on TikTok. *Social Network Analysis and Mining*, 14(227). https://doi.org/10.1007/s13278-024-01385-9

Blee, K. M. (2002). *Inside organized racism: Women in the hate movement*. University of California Press.

Blee, K. M. (2007). Women in the 1920s Ku Klux Klan movement. In B. Perry (Ed.), *Women in public and private life* (pp. 135-154). Ohio University Press.

Ecker, B., & Vaz, A. (2022). Memory reconsolidation and the crisis of mechanism in psychotherapy. *New Ideas in Psychology*, 66, 1-11. https://doi.org/10.1016/j.newideapsych.2022.100945

Frankl, V. (2010). *Man's search for meaning: The classic tribute to hope from the Holocaust*. Rider & Co.

Giddens, A. (1991). *Modernity and Self-Identity*. Polity Press.

Gillespie, A. (2020b). Semantic contact and semantic barriers: reactionary responses to disruptive ideas. *Current Opinion in Psychology*, 35, 21–25.

Gregg, G. S. (1991). *Self-representation: Life narrative studies in identity and ideology*. Greenwood Press.

Gregg, G. S. (1998). Culture, personality, and the multiplicity of identity: Evidence from North African life narratives. *Ethos*, 26(2), 120-152. https://doi.org/10.1525/eth.1998.26.2.120

Hammack, P. L. (2008). Narrative and the cultural psychology of identity. *Personality and Social Psychology Review*, 12, 222-247. https://doi.org/10.1177/1088868308316892

Hammack, P. L. (2010). Identity as burden or benefit? Youth, historical narrative, and the legacy of political conflict. *Human Development*, 53(4), 173-201. https://doi.org/10.1159/000320045

Kinnvall, C. (2004). Globalization and Religious Nationalism: Self, Identity, and the Search for Ontological Security. *Political Psychology*, 25(5), 741-767.

Kinnvall, C.; Manners, I.; Mitzen, J. (2018). Ontological (in)security in the European Union. *European Security*, 27(3), 249-265.

Kinnvall, K. & Capelos, T. (2021). The Psychology of Extremist Identification. *European Psychologist*, 26(1), 1-5. https://doi.org/10.1027/1016-9040/a000439

Kruglanski, A. W., Szumowska, E., Kopetz, C. H., Vallerand, R. J., & Pierro, A. (2021). On the psychology of extremism: How motivational imbalance breeds intemperance. *Psychological Review*, 128(2), 264–289. https://doi.org/10.1037/rev0000260

Lakoff, G. (2004). *Don't think of an elephant! Know your values and frame the debate*. Chelsea Green Publishing.

Lakoff, G. (2008). *The political mind: Why you can't understand 21st-century politics with an 18th-century brain*. Viking.

LeDoux, J. (2002). *Synaptic self: How our brains become who we are*. Penguin Viking.

McCluskey, E. (2019). *From Righteousness to Far Right: An Anthropological Rethinking of Critical Security Studies*. Montreal: McGill-Queen's University Press.

Pilkington, H. (2014). " 'My whole life is here': Tracing journeys through 'skinhead.' " In D. Buckingham, S. Bragg, and M. J. Kehily (Eds.), *Youth Cultures in the Age of Global Media* (pp. 71–87). London: Palgrave Macmillan.

Pilkington, H., Omel'chenko, E., & Garifzianova, A. (2010). *Russia's Skinheads: Exploring and rethinking subcultural lives*. London and New York: Routledge.

Quinn, N. (2006). The self. *Anthropological Theory*, 6(3), 362-384. https://doi.org/10.1177/1463499606066893

Rottmann, S., Weilnböck, H., Ghosh, S., Ricarte, J., Leitão, A., Tatalovic, S., Jasarevic, J., & Andreouli, E. (2025). *D5.2 Five Country Good Practice Case Studies Report*. OPPATTUNE Project.

Scatton, A. (2025). The "Do Associate" and "Do Not Associate" lists. ReframingAmerica.Substack.com.

Scott, J. C. (1990). *Domination and the Arts of Resistance: Hidden Transcripts*. Yale University Press.

Sen, A. (2008). Violence, identity and poverty. *Journal of Peace Research*, 45(1), 5-15. https://doi.org/10.1177/0022343307084920

Splitter, L. J. (2020). Enriching the narratives we tell about ourselves and our identities: An educational response to populism and extremism. *Educational Philosophy and Theory*, 54(1), 21-36.

Whitehouse, H. (2018). Dying for the group: Towards a general theory of extreme self-sacrifice. *Behavioral and Brain Sciences*, 41, 1–62. https://doi.org/10.1017/S0140525X18000249

Yabanci, B. (2024). Overcoming prejudices and stigmatization towards refugees: A novel approach through deliberative citizen dialogues in Turkey. Manuscript under review.

Extended Bibliography

The following comprehensive bibliography provides additional academic resources that support and expand upon the toolkit's approach. These sources represent a rich body of research on identity, narrative, extremism, and disinformation. Researchers, practitioners, and those seeking deeper understanding of the theoretical foundations of this work may find these references valuable for further exploration.

(Note: This bibliography includes works cited above plus additional relevant resources.)

Foundational Theory (Identity, Narrative, Psychology)

Atran, S. (2011). *Talking to the Enemy: Violent Extremism, Sacred Values, and What It Means to Be Human*. Penguin Books.

Bandura, A. (2002). Selective moral disengagement in the exercise of moral agency. *Journal of Moral Education*, 31(2), 101–119.

Bandura, A. (2015). *Moral disengagement: How people do harm and live with themselves*. New York: Worth Publishers.

Bar-Tal, D. (2007). Sociopsychological foundations of intractable conflicts. *American Behavioral Scientist*, 50, 1430-1453. https://doi.org/10.1177/0002764207302462

Bar-Tal, D. (2020). Conflict-supporting narratives and the struggle over them. In A. Mana & A. Srour (Eds.), *Israeli and Palestinian narratives in conflict: A tribute to Shifra Sagy and her work* (pp. 36-60). Cambridge Scholar Publishers.

Ecker, B., & Vaz, A. (2022). Memory reconsolidation and the crisis of mechanism in psychotherapy. *New Ideas in Psychology*, 66, 1-11. https://doi.org/10.1016/j.newideapsych.2022.100945

Frankl, V. (2010). *Man's search for meaning: The classic tribute to hope from the Holocaust*. Rider & Co.

Giddens, A. (1991). *Modernity and Self-Identity*. Polity Press.

Gillespie, A. (2020b). Semantic contact and semantic barriers: reactionary responses to disruptive ideas. *Current Opinion in Psychology*, 35, 21–25.

Gregg, G. S. (1991). *Self-representation: Life narrative studies in identity and ideology.* Greenwood Press.

Gregg, G. S. (1998). Culture, personality, and the multiplicity of identity: Evidence from North African life narratives. *Ethos*, 26(2), 120-152. https://doi.org/10.1525/eth.1998.26.2.120

Hammack, P. L. (2008). Narrative and the cultural psychology of identity. *Personality and Social Psychology Review*, 12, 222-247. https://doi.org/10.1177/1088868308316892

Hammack, P. L. (2010). Identity as burden or benefit? Youth, historical narrative, and the legacy of political conflict. *Human Development*, 53(4), 173-201. https://doi.org/10.1159/000320045

Kinnvall, C. (2004). Globalization and Religious Nationalism: Self, Identity, and the Search for Ontological Security. *Political Psychology*, 25(5), 741-767.

Kinnvall, C.; Manners, I.; Mitzen, J. (2018). Ontological (in)security in the European Union. *European Security*, 27(3), 249-265.

Kinnvall, K. & Capelos, T. (2021). The Psychology of Extremist Identification. *European Psychologist*, 26(1), 1-5. https://doi.org/10.1027/1016-9040/a000439

Kruglanski, A. W., Szumowska, E., Kopetz, C. H., Vallerand, R. J., & Pierro, A. (2021). On the psychology of extremism: How motivational imbalance breeds intemperance. *Psychological Review*, 128(2), 264-289. https://doi.org/10.1037/rev0000260

Lakoff, G. (2004). *Don't think of an elephant! Know your values and frame the debate*. Chelsea Green Publishing.

Lakoff, G. (2008). *The political mind: Why you can't understand 21st-century politics with an 18th-century brain*. Viking.

LeDoux, J. (2002). *Synaptic self: How our brains become who we are*. Penguin Viking.
Quinn, N. (2006). The self. *Anthropological Theory*, 6(3), 362-384. https://doi.org/10.1177/1463499606066893

Scott, J. C. (1990). *Domination and the Arts of Resistance: Hidden Transcripts*. Yale University Press.

Sen, A. (2008). Violence, identity and poverty. *Journal of Peace Research*, 45(1), 5-15. https://doi.org/10.1177/0022343307084920

Splitter, L. J. (2020). Enriching the narratives we tell about ourselves and our identities: An educational response to populism and extremism. *Educational Philosophy and Theory*, 54(1), 21-36.

Whitehouse, H. (2018). Dying for the group: Towards a general theory of extreme self-sacrifice. *Behavioral and Brain Sciences*, 41, 1–62. https://doi.org/10.1017/S0140525X18000249

Counter-Narrative & Alternative Narrative Research

Allchorn, W. (2020). Building a successful radical right counter-narrative campaign: A how-to guide. Retrieved from: https://www.hedayahcent

Appel, M., & Richter, T. (2007). Persuasive effects of fictional narratives increase over time. Media Psychology, 10(1), 113-134.

Awan, A., Miskimmon, A., & O'Loughlin, B. (2019). The battle for the battle of the narratives: Sidestepping the double fetish of digital and CVE. In C. Bjola & J. Pamment (Eds.), Countering online propaganda and extremism: The dark side of digital diplomacy (pp. 156-171). Routledge.

Braddock, K. (2020). Weaponized words: The strategic role of persuasion in violent radicalization and counter-radicalization. Cambridge University Press.

Braddock, K., & Horgan, J. (2016). Towards a guide for constructing and disseminating counternarratives to reduce support for terrorism. Studies in Conflict & Terrorism, 39(5), 381-404.

Braddock, K., & Dillard, J. (2016). Meta-analytic evidence for the persuasive effect of narratives on beliefs, attitudes, intentions, and behaviors. Communication Monographs, 83(4), 446-467.

Briggs, R., & Feve, S. (2013). Review of programs to counter narratives of violent extremism: What works and what are the implications for government? Retrieved from: https://www.dhs.gov/

Butcher, P., & Neidhardt, A. (2020). Fear and lying in the EU: Fighting disinformation on migration with alternative narratives. European Migration and Diversity Programme.

Frischlich, L., Rieger, D., Morten, A., & Bente, G. (2018). The power of a good story: Narrative persuasion in extremist propaganda and videos against violent extremism. International Journal of Conflict and Violence, 12, 1-17.

Hedayah. (2014). Developing effective counter-narrative frameworks for countering violent extremism. Retrieved from: http://www.icct.nl/

Juntunen, M., & Ruohomäki, O. (2024). Alternative narratives and countering violent extremism in the arc of instability: Reflections on post-ISIS Iraq. In P. Uusikylä, H. Jalonen, & A. Jokipii (Eds.), Information resilience and comprehensive security. Information technology and global governance. Palgrave Macmillan.

Kruglova, A. (2020). I will tell you a story about jihad: ISIS propaganda and narrative advertising. Studies in Conflict and Terrorism, 44(2), 115-137.

Kruglova, A. (2022). Terrorist recruitment, propaganda and branding: Selling terror online. Routledge.

Meleagrou-Hitchens, A. (2017). The challenges and limitations of online counter-narratives in the fight against ISIS recruitment in Europe and North America. Georgetown Journal of International Affairs, 18(3), 95-104.

Monaci, S. (2020). Social media campaigns against violent extremism: A new approach to evaluating video storytelling. International Journal of Communication, 14, 980-1003.

Pretus, C., Javeed, A. M., Hughes, D., Hackenburg, K., Tsakiris, M., Vilarroya, O., & Van Bavel, J. J. (2024). The misleading count: An identity-based intervention to counter partisan misinformation sharing. Philosophical Transactions of the Royal Society.

Ramakrishna, K., Morales, Y. R. S., & Renomeron-Morales, S. (2021). Countering violent Islamist extremism in Muslim Mindanao the 4M way: The role of alternative narratives. Studies in Conflict & Terrorism, 46(12), 2538-2563.

Ruston, S. W., & Halverson, J. R. (2014). Counter or alternative: Visual propaganda and extremism in the online environment. US Army College: Strategic Studies Institute.

Schlegel, L. (2021). Storytelling against extremism: How fiction could increase the persuasive impact of counter- and alternative narratives in P/CVE. Journal of Deradicalization, 27, 193-237.

Schmid, A. (2014). Al-Qaeda's "single narrative" and attempts to de-velop counter-narratives: The state of knowledge. The Hague: International Centre for Counter-Terrorism.

Extremism, Culture, and Context

Andreouli, E., Ghosh, S., Ricarte, J., Rottmann, S., Weilnböck, H., & Leitão, A. (2024). *D5.1 Framework paper on emergence of opposition drivers across sites and shared dialogical interventions*. OPPATTUNE Project.

Bhattacharya, S., Agarwal, N., & Poudel, D. (2024). Analyzing the impact of symbols in Taiwan's election-related anti-disinformation campaign on TikTok. *Social Network Analysis and Mining*, 14(227). https://doi.org/10.1007/s13278-024-01385-9

Blee, K. M. (2002). *Inside organized racism: Women in the hate movement*. University of California Press.

Blee, K. M. (2007). Women in the 1920s Ku Klux Klan movement. In B. Perry (Ed.), *Women in public and private life* (pp. 135-154). Ohio University Press.

Buhrmester, M. D., Zeitlyn, D., & Whitehouse, H. (2020). Ritual, fusion, and conflict: The roots of agro-pastoral violence in rural Cameroon. *Group Processes & Intergroup Relations*, 25(1), 298–311. https://doi.org/10.1177/1368430220959705

Ebner, J., Kavanagh, C., & Whitehouse, H. (2022). Is There a Language of Terrorists? A Comparative Manifesto Analysis. *Studies in Conflict & Terrorism*, 1-26. https://doi.org/10.1080/1057610X.2022.2064908

Kavanagh, C., Wibisono, S., Kapitány, R., Yustisia, W., Putra, I. E., Rufaedah, A., & Whitehouse, H. (2019). Exploring the role of identity fusion and group identification in predicting parochialism amongst Indonesian Islamic groups. *PsyArXiv*. https://doi.org/10.31234/osf.io/sjht4

McCluskey, E. (2019). *From Righteousness to Far Right: An Anthropological Rethinking of Critical Security Studies*. Montreal: McGill-Queen's University Press.

Newson, M. (2019). Football, fan violence, and identity fusion. *International Review for the Sociology of Sport*, 54(4), 431–444. https://doi.org/10.1177/1012690217731293

Newson, M., Bortolini, T., Buhrmester, M., da Silva, S. R., Queiroga da Aquino, J. N., & Whitehouse, H. (2018). Brazil's Football Warriors: Social bonding and inter-group violence. *Evolution and Human Behaviour*, 39(6), 675–683. https://doi.org/10.1016/j.evolhumbehav.2018.06.010

Pilkington, H. (2014). " 'My whole life is here': Tracing journeys through 'skinhead.' " In D. Buckingham, S. Bragg, and M. J. Kehily (Eds.), *Youth Cultures in the Age of Global Media* (pp. 71–87). London: Palgrave Macmillan.

Pilkington, H., Omel'chenko, E., & Garifzianova, A. (2010). *Russia's Skinheads: Exploring and rethinking subcultural lives*. London and New York: Routledge.

Rottmann, S., Weilnböck, H., Ghosh, S., Ricarte, J., Leitão, A., Tatalovic, S., Jasarevic, J., & Andreouli, E. (2025). *D5.2 Five Country Good Practice Case Studies Report*. OPPATTUNE Project.

Whitehouse, H., McQuinn, B., Buhrmester, M., & Swann, W. B. (2014). Brothers in arms: Warriors bond like family. *Proceedings of the Na-*

tional Academy of Sciences, 111(50), 17783–17785. https://doi.org/10.1073/pnas.1416284111

Whitehouse, H., Jong, J., Buhrmester, M. D., Gómez, Á., Bastian, B., Kavanagh, C. M., Newson, M., Matthews, M., Lanman, J. A., McKay, R., & Gavrilets, S. (2017). The evolution of extreme cooperation via shared dysphoric experiences. *Scientific Reports*, 7, 1–10. https://doi.org/10.1038/srep44292

Framing, Disinformation & Policy

Scatton, A. (2025). The "Do Associate" and "Do Not Associate" lists. ReframingAmerica.Substack.com

11 Glossary of Terms

- **Agency**: The feeling of being in control of your own life and choices.
- **Backfire Effect**: The phenomenon where directly confronting someone's deeply held beliefs (even false ones) can make them cling to those beliefs even more strongly.
- **Belonging**: The feeling of being connected to a group and accepted by others. A fundamental human need.
- **Practical Guide / This Toolkit**: This document! A guide designed to empower individuals and community members to take action against IBD.
- **Co-option**: When an IBD agent adopts the language or imagery of a positive message but twists it to support their own agenda.
- **Continuity**: The feeling of connection to the past, present, and future; having a sense of history and tradition.
- **Counter-Narrative**: See "Alternative Narrative" or "Equal Alternative Narrative" (preferred term).
- **Echo Chamber**: An environment (often online) where people are primarily exposed to information that confirms their existing beliefs, reinforcing biases.
- **Equal Alternative Narrative**: A positive message or story that addresses the same underlying needs as an IBD narrative but does so in a healthy, inclusive, and constructive way. The term

"equal" refers specifically to matching the *psychological effectiveness* and *need-fulfillment capacity* of the IBD, **not** implying moral or factual equivalence. This is the preferred term over "counter-narrative."

- **False Choice** (or **False Dichotomy**): A situation where someone is presented with only two options, when in reality, more options exist. IBD often uses false choices to manipulate people.
- **Gaslighting**: A form of manipulation where someone tries to make you doubt your own perceptions or sanity.
- **Guilt by Association**: A tactic where someone tries to discredit a message by associating it with a disliked person or group.
- **Hashtag**: A word or phrase preceded by a "#" symbol, used on social media to categorize and find content.
- **Hook, Line, and Sinker**: A strategy for sequencing social media posts to build engagement: - Hook: An attention-grabbing post - Line: Posts that provide more context and information - Sinker: Posts that directly address underlying needs and values
- **Identity**: The sense of who you are, including your values, beliefs, group affiliations, and cultural heritage.
- **Identity-Based Disinformation (IBD)**: A harmful form of manipulation that targets people's sense of identity to sow division, erode trust, and undermine social cohesion.
- **Misinformation**: False or inaccurate information, regardless of intent.
- **Disinformation**: False information that is deliberately spread to deceive or mislead.
- **Narrative**: A story or account of events, experiences, or be-

liefs.

- **"Other" Group**: In the context of IBD, the group being portrayed negatively in the disinformation. This toolkit focuses on strengthening the target audience, not directly addressing the "Other" group.
- **Positive Identity Expansion**: The core strategy of this toolkit. It involves broadening and strengthening the target audience's sense of identity, making them more resilient to IBD.
- **Red Teaming**: The practice of thinking like an opponent to identify weaknesses in your own plan.
- **Resilience**: The ability to withstand and recover from difficult situations. In this context, resilience to IBD.
- **Security**: The feeling of being safe and protected. A fundamental human need.
- **Self-Esteem**: The feeling of being good about oneself and one's place in the world. A fundamental human need.
- **Significance**: The feeling that one's life has meaning and purpose. A fundamental human need.
- **Social Cohesion**: The degree to which members of a community or society are connected and work together.
- **Straw Man Argument**: Misrepresenting someone's argument to make it easier to attack.
- **Target Audience**: The group of people the IBD creators are trying to influence. They are the ones receiving the manipulative messages. This toolkit focuses on empowering the target audience.
- **Trusted Voices**: Individuals or organizations that are respected and listened to by the target audience.
- **Whataboutism**: Deflecting criticism by pointing to a different,

unrelated issue.

12 Join the Community: Contributing to the Toolkit

This toolkit is designed to be a living resource, evolving and improving through the collective wisdom and experience of its users. We believe that by working together, we can make these tools even more effective in countering identity-based disinformation and fostering positive narratives.

Why Collaborate?

Your insights are invaluable:

Sharing Experiences: How have you used these methods? What worked? What challenges did you face? Sharing your story helps others learn.

Improving Content: Have you spotted an error, an unclear explanation, or an area that could be improved? Let us know!

Adding Resources: Do you know of other helpful organizations, readings, case studies, or resources? Help us expand the Related Organizations and Resources section.

Diverse Perspectives: Contributions from people with diverse backgrounds and experiences make the toolkit stronger and more relevant globally.

The Public Repository: Our Collaboration Hub

To facilitate this collaboration, a public project repository is hosted on GitHub and maintained independantly:

https://github.com/counteribd/reclaiming-our-narrative/

GitHub is a platform widely used for collaborative projects, especially in software development, but it's also great for managing shared documents like this toolkit. It allows us to track changes, discuss ideas, and integrate contributions smoothly.

How You Can Contribute (All Skill Levels Welcome!)

You don't need to be a technical expert to contribute! Here are several ways to get involved:

Easiest Ways (No Technical Skills Needed):

- **Suggest Improvements or Report Errors:** If you find a typo, a broken link, something unclear, or have an idea for improvement, the easiest way to let us know is by creating an "Issue" on GitHub. Think of it like leaving a suggestion note. Go to the repository link above, find the "Issues" tab, and click "New Issue".

- **Share Your Experiences & Ask Questions:** Have you used the toolkit? Want to discuss a concept or share how it worked in your community? Use the "Discussions" tab on GitHub (if enabled) to start or join conversations. This is a great place for broader dialogue.
- **Propose New Resources:** Found a great article, organization, or case study that should be included? Create an "Issue" describing the resource and why it's relevant.

More Involved Contributions (Using GitHub):

For those comfortable with GitHub's workflow (or willing to learn!), you can contribute directly to the toolkit's content:

1. **Understand the Basics:** Familiarize yourself with the standard GitHub process: Forking the repository, creating a branch for your changes, making edits, and submitting a Pull Request (PR).
2. **Follow Guidelines:** Please review our detailed Contributing Guidelines for specifics on formatting, style, and the PR process.
3. **Examples:** You could add a new case study using the template, improve a worksheet, add to the recommended reading list, or even help translate the toolkit.

Respectful Collaboration

All participation in this project is governed by our Code of Conduct. We are committed to maintaining a welcoming, respectful, and inclusive environment for everyone.

We look forward to building this resource together!

We believe in making the tools to reclaim narratives widely accessible. There are many ways you can support the OICD's mission and help sustain this important work. Sharing the open access PDF version (available at oicd.net/resources) with friends or colleagues, contributing to the toolkit's development (as detailed above), or purchasing print or e-book copies are all invaluable ways to help. Thank you for being part of this crucial effort to counter identity-based disinformation.

13 Organizations and Resources for Countering IBD

Organizations Researching and Countering Identity-Based Disinformation

The fight against identity-based disinformation involves a diverse ecosystem of actors operating at international, regional, national, and local levels. This section categorizes organizations by geographic scope, highlighting their specific relevance to IBD.

International Organizations

Global bodies play a crucial role in setting norms, coordinating efforts, and providing resources to address disinformation and IBD worldwide.

- **Organization for Identity & Cultural Development (OICD)**

    - Website: oicd.net

    - Description: Developers of this toolkit, the OICD develops evidence-based methods to understand and address identity-based conflict and manipulation.

This guide is a practical application for the general reader derived from the OICD's comprehensive **EMIC (Engagement Methodology for Identities in Conflict)** methodology. The OICD offers further resources and professional training programs for organizations, practitioners, and researchers interested in mastering the full EMIC method for deeper, scalable analysis and intervention design.

– The OICD can provide enhanced AI prompts and scalable software-based solutions for organizations and agencies.

– The OICD's National Response, Prevention & Resilience program can produce and coordinate counter IBD campaigns across national populations.

• **UNESCO (United Nations Educational, Scientific and Cultural Organization)**

   – Website: https://www.unesco.org/en/countering-hate-speech

   – Description: UNESCO tackles hate speech through education, media and information literacy (MIL), promoting international standards on freedom of expression, and supporting member states in building effective responses. It addresses various forms of intolerance, including xenophobia, racism, antisemitism, anti-Muslim hatred, anti-LGBTQI+ hatred, and misogyny, recognizing their proliferation via social media. UNESCO directly counters identity-based hate through targeted educational guides for policymakers and teachers, MIL initiatives like the MIL Alliance and campaigns (#ThinkBeforeSharing), and resources addressing specific forms like antisemitism and gender-based violence online. Its work operates within the framework of the broader UN Strategy and Plan of Action on Hate Speech.

- **UN Office on Genocide Prevention and the Responsibility to Protect (OSAPG)**

  - Website: https://www.un.org/en/genocideprevention/hate-speech.shtml

  - Description: Serves as the UN system's focal point for implementing the UN Strategy and Plan of Action on Hate Speech, launched in 2019. The office works to address the root causes and drivers of hate speech, monitor its manifestations, support victims, and engage with technology companies. Crucially, it analyzes the dangerous links between hate speech targeting specific identity groups and the potential risk of atrocity crimes, including genocide. OSAPG plays a central role in coordinating UN efforts against hate speech targeting groups based on religion, ethnicity, nationality, race, colour, descent, gender, or other identity factors. It develops crucial guidance documents and training materials on the UN Strategy, including specific guidance for media stakeholders, religious leaders, and addressing phenomena like COVID-19 related hate speech. Its analysis explicitly connects identity-based hate speech to the prevention of the most severe international crimes.

- **UNICRI (United Nations Interregional Crime and Justice Research Institute)**

  – Website: https://unicri.org/

  – Description: Conducts research on crime prevention and justice. This includes examining the malicious use of social media by terrorist, violent extremist, and criminal groups, particularly how these actors exploit online platforms to spread their narratives and undermine trust. UNICRI noted a significant increase in the exploitation of social media for extremist narratives and conspiracy theories during crises like the COVID-19 pandemic. It has launched a Centre on Disinformation, though its initial public focus has been on Chemical, Biological, Radiological, and Nuclear (CBRN) disinformation. UNICRI's research explicitly connects the use of social media by extremist and terrorist groups to the reinforcement of narratives designed to manipulate populations, often leveraging identity factors. While the current public emphasis of its Disinformation Centre is on CBRN threats, the Institute's underlying analysis of how extremist groups exploit platforms to propagate harmful narratives is highly relevant to understanding broader identity-based disinformation tactics. UNICRI also offers related training, such as its Summer School on Misinformation, Disinformation and Hate Speech.

- **UNFPA (United Nations Population Fund)**

- Website: https://www.unfpa.org/

- Description: Specifically addresses gendered hate speech online, with a particular emphasis on the proliferation of misogynistic hate speech targeting women and girls.   UNFPA participates in global partnerships aimed at tackling online gender-based harassment and abuse and has issued guidance on the safe and ethical use of technology in relation to gender-based violence. UNFPA brings a critical focus to gender and misogyny as specific, virulent forms of identity-based hate speech spreading online.   Its work highlights the connection between online hate targeting women and girls and real-world discrimination, inequality, and violence, underscoring the tangible harms of IBD.

European Organizations

Europe has developed a dense network of institutions and organizations focused on monitoring and countering disinformation and hate speech within the region.

- **Council of Europe (CoE)**

    - Website: https://www.coe.int/en/web/combating-hate-speech/home

    - Description: A key intergovernmental organization promoting human rights, democracy, and the rule of law across Europe.   It combats hate speech through various mechanisms, including setting legal standards, monitoring compliance via bodies like the European Commission against Racism and Intolerance (ECRI), parliamentary initiatives such as the No Hate Parliamentary Alliance, and leveraging its human rights mechanisms like the European Court of Human Rights (ECtHR) and the Commissioner for Human Rights. Its work addresses racism, intolerance, and discrimination based on diverse grounds. The CoE is central to establishing norms and providing resources against identity-based hate in Europe. It develops key policy instruments like Recommendation CM/Rec(2022)16 on Combating Hate Speech. Its online Knowledge Hub provides access to standards and resources, including tools developed by civil society organizations (CSOs) targeting specific forms of hate like anti-Muslim hate, anti-LGBTI hate, and hate speech directed at women journalists. The CoE promotes initiatives like the No Hate Speech Week, and the jurisprudence of the ECtHR provides legal precedents regarding hate speech targeting specific population groups.

- **EUvsDisinfo (EEAS East StratCom Task Force)**

  - Website: https://euvsdisinfo.eu/

  - Description: The flagship project of the European External Action Service (EEAS) dedicated to identifying, analyzing, debunking, and raising awareness about pro-Kremlin disinformation campaigns. Its scope covers campaigns targeting the EU, its Member States, the Eastern Neighbourhood, the Western Balkans, Sub-Saharan Africa and other global partners. A core component is its large, publicly accessible database documenting thousands of disinformation cases. It also addresses the broader concept of Foreign Information Manipulation and Interference (FIMI). The EUvsDisinfo database serves as a critical resource for observing how pro-Kremlin sources utilize identity-related narratives. It contains numerous examples of disinformation targeting migrants, Muslims, Jews, and LGBTQ+ individuals, or manipulating historical narratives linked to national or ethnic identity. The project publishes regular analyses and educational materials explaining disinformation tactics, including those that exploit identity fault lines. Significantly, it collaborated with EU DisinfoLab on developing practical guidelines for investigating IBD-focused FIMI.

- **EDMO (European Digital Media Observatory)**

  - Website: https://edmo.eu/

  - Description: An independent observatory acting as a hub connecting fact-checkers, academic researchers, and media literacy experts across Europe to strengthen the fight against disinformation. EDMO provides access to resources, supports a network of national and regional hubs, and facilitates researcher access to platform data. EDMO's repositories of fact-checks and research publications contain significant analysis of identity-based disinformation trends prevalent across

Europe. By connecting diverse experts, it fosters a more comprehensive understanding of how IBD manifests in different national contexts. Furthermore, its support for media literacy initiatives is crucial for building public resilience against all forms of manipulative content, including IBD, and its policy analysis informs efforts to regulate the digital spaces where IBD proliferates.

- **EU DisinfoLab**

  - Website: https://www.disinfo.eu/

  - Description: An independent, non-profit organization based in Brussels that specializes in researching disinformation across Europe. It employs investigative techniques like Open Source Intelligence (OSINT), network analysis, and develops policy recommendations. EU DisinfoLab actively shares knowledge and convenes the counter-disinformation community through events and publications. EU DisinfoLab has demonstrated a specific focus on *identity-based* disinformation. It has produced resources explicitly aimed at detecting and analyzing IBD within the context of FIMI, including a notable OSINT toolkit developed in collaboration with the EEAS. Their work signifies the growing recognition of IBD as a distinct area requiring specialized investigative methods.

- **Institute for Strategic Dialogue (ISD)**

  - Website: https://www.isdglobal.org/

- Description: A global 'think and do' tank dedicated to research and policy development to counter extremism, hate, polarization, and disinformation. It utilizes a Digital Analysis Unit to understand and respond to online threats globally. ISD demonstrates a particularly strong focus on identity-based issues. Its program areas explicitly include Islamophobia, Antisemitism, Misogyny, Anti-LGBTQ+ hate, Far-Right Extremism, and Islamism. ISD regularly publishes specific, in-depth reports analyzing phenomena such as gendered online abuse targeting women in politics, hate speech tactics used against specific ethnic or religious groups, and the identity-based underpinnings of various extremist ideologies.

- **Center for Countering Digital Hate (CCDH)**

  - Website: https://counterhate.com/

  - Description: A non-governmental organization with operations in the UK and US, focused on disrupting the architecture of online hate and misinformation. CCDH achieves this through research exposing harmful actors and platform failures, public campaigns to galvanize pressure, and policy advocacy aimed at increasing plat-form accountability. CCDH's research and campaigns frequently target specific forms of identity-based hate, including documented work on antisemitism, misog-yny (e.g., investigating incel communities, analyzing violence against women online), and potentially other forms. A key aspect of their work involves investigating how platform algorithms can amplify harmful identity-related content, such as their research on YouTube recommending eating disorder content to young girls. They also offer practical resources like resilience training to help individuals and organizations navigate online hate.

- **HOPE not hate**

    – Website: https://www.hopenothate.org.uk/

    – Description: A UK-based advocacy group and charity that monitors and actively challenges far-right extremism and racism. It combines research with community intelligence and engagement activities, particularly in areas susceptible to divisive narratives. Its flagship publication is the annual "State of Hate" report. HOPE not hate directly confronts extremist ideologies that are fundamentally built upon identity-based hatred, including racism, anti-immigrant sentiment, anti-Muslim hostility, and anti-LGBTQ+ prejudice. Its research seeks to understand the drivers of hate and extremism within communities, which inherently involves analyzing how identity factors are manipulated and exploited.

- **Community Security Trust (CST)**

    – Website: https://cst.org.uk/

- Description: An organization dedicated to protecting the Jewish community in the UK from antisemitism and related security threats. Its activities include monitoring antisemitic incidents, providing security advice and training, and offering expertise on anti-Jewish hate and disinformation. CST possesses deep, specialized expertise specifically focused on antisemitism, a significant and persistent form of identity-based hate and disinformation. While its primary focus is the Jewish community, its operational model for community-specific monitoring, incident recording, and response provides a valuable example.

- **Glitch**

  - Website: https://glitchcharity.co.uk/

  - Description: A UK-based charity working to end online abuse and create safer digital spaces, with a particular focus on the experiences of Black women and other marginalized groups. It employs campaigning, training, and resource development, including its own digital self-defence toolkit, to promote digital citizenship and tech justice. Glitch explicitly centers its work on the intersection of race and gender in the context of online abuse and safety. It addresses how algorithmic bias and technological design can disproportionately harm marginalized identities. Its resources and training are tailored to equip individuals from these communities with tools for digital self-defence against identity-based attacks.

- **HATEDEMICS Project**

    - Description: An EU-funded research project operating under the Horizon Europe programme, involving a consortium of 14 partners across Europe, including NGOs, public authorities, and research institutions. The project aims to develop and deploy AI-assisted tools to help practitioners (NGOs, activists, fact-checkers) combat online polarization, hate speech, and disinformation more effectively, using a human-in-the-loop approach for generating counter-speech. HATEDEMICS directly addresses the critical intersection where hate speech and disinformation converge, a nexus frequently characterized by the targeting of specific identities. By seeking to empower NGOs and activists who are often on the front lines of combating identity-based hate online, the project aims to provide practical technological support for countering these specific harms.

- **ATHENA Project**

    - Description: Another Horizon Europe project concentrating on enhancing Europe's defence against Foreign Information Manipulation and Interference (FIMI). Its objectives include the early detection of FIMI campaigns, a better understanding of their behavioural and societal impacts, and assessing the effectiveness of countermeasures deployed before, during, and after such campaigns. Given that FIMI campaigns frequently employ identity-based narratives as a core tactic to achieve their manipulative goals, ATHENA's research into FIMI detection methodologies, impact assessment, and countermeasure effectiveness is inherently relevant to understanding and developing strategies against IBD, particularly when it manifests as part of coordinated, state-linked influence operations.

North American Organizations

Several prominent organizations based in North America are leaders in tracking extremism, hate crimes, and disinformation, often with a strong focus on identity-based issues.

- **Anti-Defamation League (ADL) & Center on Extremism (COE)**

  - Website: https://www.adl.org/

  - Description: Founded in the US, the ADL is an international NGO combating antisemitism and all forms of prejudice and discrimination. Its Center on Extremism (COE) functions as its research arm, recognized as a foremost authority on extremism, terrorism, and hate, monitoring groups and ideologies across the political spectrum, both domestic and foreign. COE provides resources, expertise, and training to law enforcement, public officials, community leaders, and technology companies. The ADL also operates a Center for Technology and Society focused on online hate. The ADL/COE is a primary source for data and analysis on antisemitism.

Its remit extends to tracking a wide range of extremist ideologies, including white supremacy, which are inherently identity-based. COE offers several indispensable resources for understanding the manifestations of identity-based hate: the H.E.A.T. Map visually tracks specific incidents of hate, extremism, antisemitism, and terrorism across the US; the Hate Symbols Database is a critical reference for identifying symbols used by extremist groups; and the Glossary of Extremism and Hate defines key terms and profiles individuals/groups. They publish timely reports on trends, such as analysis of white supremacist propaganda targeting Jews and immigrants, or investigations into bias within AI models.

- **Southern Poverty Law Center (SPLC) & Hatewatch**

  - Website: https://www.splcenter.org/

  - Description: A US non-profit legal advocacy organization renowned for monitoring hate groups and extremist activities, with a particular focus on the hard right. Its Hatewatch program serves as a blog and monitoring initiative exposing these activities. Key outputs include the annual "Year in Hate & Extremism" report and the interactive Hate Map. A core mission is dismantling white supremacy. SPLC provides extensive tracking and reporting on a wide array of identity-based hate groups, including white nationalist, neo-Nazi, anti-immigrant, anti-LGBTQ+, and anti-Muslim organizations. The Hate Map offers a visual representation of the geographic distribution of these groups. Hatewatch articles pro-vide detailed exposés of specific activities, rhetoric, and campaigns targeting various identities, such as investigations into antisemitic podcast hosts, analysis of anti-LGBTQ+ 'natural family' rhetoric with racist roots, or reporting on anti-immigrant narratives. (It is worth noting that the SPLC's focus has drawn criticism from some quarters for being perceived as exclusively targeting right-wing groups).

- **Polarization and Extremism Research and Innovation Lab (PERIL) at American University**

  - Website: https://www.american.edu/spa/peril/

  - Description: An academic research lab dedicated to developing and testing evidence-based strategies and tools aimed at preventing radicalization and countering mis/disinformation. Its work specifically examines the intersection of extremism, identity, and online environments, employing a public health approach focused on pre-prevention and resilience building. PERIL's research directly addresses *identity-based* radicalization processes. It creates practical resources such as toolkits, guides, media literacy interventions, short-form videos, and training programs specifically designed to build community resilience against extremist propaganda that targets and manipulates identity. A key principle of its work is centering the needs and perspectives of groups targeted by hate and extremism.

- **Strong Cities Network (SCN)**

    - Website: https://strongcitiesnetwork.org/

    - Description: A global network connecting mayors, city-
      level policymakers, and local practitioners committed
      to preventing and countering hate, extremism, and
      polarization within urban environments. SCN facilitates
      peer learning, knowledge sharing, and capacity-building
      efforts tailored to the needs of local governments. SCN
      provides practical guidance specifically for cities on how
      to address hate speech and its connections to extremism.
      This includes strategies for identifying and tracking hate
      speech (using technology, community partnerships, and
      monitoring), strengthening community partnerships
      for reporting, consistent public messaging from city
      leaders, implementing clear local policies, promoting
      multi-actor coordination, investing in education and
      media literacy, and upskilling local authorities and
      front-line practitioners. Its Resource Hub contains tools
      and guides for addressing identity-based hate as it
      manifests within local communities. The network also
      offers tailored considerations for mayors responding to
      hate speech during times of crisis, when such rhetoric
      often escalates.

- **American Library Association (ALA) - Office for Intellectual Freedom (OIF) & Office for Diversity, Literacy and
  Outreach Services (ODLOS)**

- Website: https://www.ala.org/advocacy/intfreedom/ha
te

- Description: These offices within the ALA provide
guidance, resources, and support to libraries across
the US grappling with issues of hateful conduct, hate
speech, bias, and discrimination, while simultaneously
upholding principles of intellectual freedom. Libraries
serve as vital community hubs and public spaces where
issues of identity-based hate and disinformation often
surface. The ALA offices offer practical resources, such
as a white paper on "Hateful Conduct in Libraries", advis-
ing libraries on policy development, First Amendment
considerations, and professional ethics. They encourage libraries to use their institutional voice to actively
counter messages of bias and discrimination through
programming and services and provide direct support
for library staff who encounter or are impacted by hate
speech. They represent an important community-level
resource network addressing these challenges.

Other Relevant Actors

Beyond dedicated counter-disinformation organizations or those
focused on specific regions, other entities contribute valuable
perspectives and resources.

- **ARTICLE 19**

    - Website: https://www.article19.org/

- Description: An international human rights organization with a global mandate to defend and promote freedom of expression and the right to information. Its work encompasses issues such as censorship, digital rights, media freedom, the safety of journalists, and platform accountability. ARTICLE 19 consistently addresses online hate speech and disinformation within a robust human rights and freedom of expression framework. Its research delves into digital repression tactics, including surveillance technologies that disproportionately target marginalized groups. The organization actively works to protect journalists, recognizing that attacks against them are often identity-based (e.g., gendered or racist abuse). It analyzes information integrity challenges in conflict zones, where identity is frequently weaponized, and provides critical analysis of social media content moderation practices and intermediary liability issues pertinent to the spread and control of IBD.

- **Hybrid CoE (European Centre of Excellence for Countering Hybrid Threats)**

  - Website: https://www.hybridcoe.fi/

  - Description: An international hub based in Helsinki, supported by NATO and the EU, dedicated to fostering strategic understanding, research, and cooperation among participating states on countering hybrid threats. The Hybrid CoE produces strategic analyses examining how identity markers—such as gender, race/ethnicity, sexual orientation, class—are deliberately exploited within disinformation campaigns as a component of broader hybrid threat activities. Their research illuminates how adversaries manipulate existing social divisions and power dynamics linked to identity to provoke conflict, undermine trust, and destabilize democratic societies. This includes analyzing the use of emotional narratives targeting identity-linked values and wedge issues.

This list of organizations highlights the multifaceted nature of the challenge and the corresponding diversity of actors involved. It underscores that effectively tackling IBD requires drawing on expertise from international standard-setters, regional bodies focused on specific threats (like pro-Kremlin disinformation), national monitoring groups, academic researchers, local government networks, and human rights advocates. A clear pattern emerges: no single entity possesses all the answers or tools. Instead, a collaborative, multi-stakeholder approach, involving governments, international organizations, technology companies, civil society, academia, media, and individuals, is consistently identified as essential for developing comprehensive and effective responses.

Essential Resources: Databases, Reports, and Toolkits

This section details specific databases, flagship reports, practical toolkits, and educational materials offered by prominent players, maintaining a clear focus on their utility for understanding and countering *identity-based* disinformation.

EUvsDisinfo Deep Dive (EEAS StratCom)

The EUvsDisinfo project, managed by the EEAS East StratCom Task Force, provides a wealth of resources specifically focused on pro-Kremlin disinformation, much of which involves identity manipulation.

- **Disinformation Database:**

  - **Description:** This is a cornerstone resource—a searchable, open-source repository containing records of thousands of individual disinformation cases attributed to pro-Kremlin outlets since 2015. Each entry typically includes the specific disinformation claim alongside a brief disproof, context, or link to further information. The database is updated weekly, ensuring timeliness, though its primary interface and case descriptions are available only in English.

  - **Relevance to IBD:** The database is invaluable for observing and documenting how pro-Kremlin sources weaponize identity. Users can search using keywords related to specific identity groups (e.g., "migrants," "Muslims," "Jewish," "LGBT," "gender," specific nationalities like "Ukrainian") to uncover examples of how these identities are framed within disinformation narratives. This provides concrete, searchable evidence of identity exploitation tactics used in real-world campaigns. Analysis of the database content reveals recurring narratives targeting migrants/Muslims as threats (cultural, criminal, economic), deploying antisemitic tropes, or distorting historical events linked to national identity. Keywords indexed within the database confirm the presence of themes like migration, religion (Muslims, Catholic Church, Christianity), antisemitism (implied via Holocaust denial/distortion, figures like Soros, specific leaders like Netanyahu), gender issues, specific national-ities/ethnicities (Crimean Tatars, Chechens, Ukrainians), and historical revisionism aimed at undermining na-tional identities.

- **Reports & Analysis:**

  - **Description:** Beyond the database, EUvsDisinfo pub-lishes regular "Disinformation Reviews" that synthesize recent trends and narratives. They also produce in-depth reports analyzing specific, high-profile dis-information campaigns (such as those surrounding the downing of flight MH17 or the Skripal poisoning), detailed analyses of FIMI tactics and the architecture of influence operations, and articles focusing on particular themes or geographic regions (e.g., disinformation targeting Georgia or emanating from China). An online library also curates relevant external studies and reports.

  - **Relevance to IBD:** The analytical outputs frequently dissect narratives targeting specific countries, minori-ties, or social groups. Reports examining FIMI tactics are directly relevant, as these coordinated influence op-erations often rely heavily on exploiting identity-based divisions. Specific reports have utilized EUvsDisinfo data to analyze campaigns targeting migrants and minorities within the EU. Furthermore, the collaboration with EU DisinfoLab on OSINT guidelines for investigating IBD-focused FIMI demonstrates a commitment to addressing this specific threat vector.

- **Educational Materials ("Learn" Section):**

  - **Description:** This section of the EUvsDisinfo website serves as an educational hub. It provides clear definitions of essential terminology (distinguishing disinformation from misinformation, defining FIMI, etc.). It explains core disinformation narratives, explicitly including sections on "Hate Speech" and "Conspiracy Theories," and discusses common rhetorical devices employed by manipulators. The section aims to equip users with tools and resources—including articles, videos, games, and podcasts—to build personal and societal resilience against manipulation.

  - **Relevance to IBD:** The explicit inclusion of "Hate Speech" and "Conspiracy Theories" as key narrative types directly addresses phenomena heavily intertwined with identity targeting. By explaining how narratives are constructed and the rhetorical tricks used, this section helps users deconstruct how identity is woven into manipulative messaging. The overarching goal is to help citizens recognize and resist information manipulation, including sophisticated campaigns that exploit identity-based vulnerabilities.

EDMO Resource Summary

The European Digital Media Observatory (EDMO) acts as a central node connecting various actors and resources across Europe.

- **Fact-Checking:** EDMO provides access to a repository of fact-checking articles, investigative briefs, a map highlighting notable fact-checks, and a list of fact-checking organizations operating within the EU. *Relevance to IBD:* Given the prevalence of IBD in Europe, the fact-checks cataloged by EDMO frequently address disinformation targeting identity groups such as migrants, religious minorities, and others. This provides users with verified information countering specific false narratives.

- **Research:** The platform includes a repository for scientific publications related to disinformation, facilitates researcher access to platform data, and lists relevant CSOs and academic institutions. *Relevance to IBD:* The academic research curated by EDMO contains numerous studies analyzing identity-based disinformation trends, their societal impacts, and potential countermeasures within the specific European context. Access to platform data is crucial for researchers investigating the spread and amplification of IBD online.

- **Media Literacy:** EDMO offers resources like a media literacy overview, guidelines for practitioners ("Raising Standards: The EDMO Guidelines"), a dedicated digest, a mapping of existing initiatives, and a training program. *Relevance to IBD:* Enhancing media literacy is a fundamental strategy for building resilience against all forms of disinformation, including

IBD. EDMO's resources support educators and practitioners in developing effective programs that equip citizens with critical thinking skills needed to navigate identity-based manipulation.

- **Reports & Analysis:** EDMO publishes periodic insights and early warnings on emerging disinformation trends, provides policy analysis (including on the EU Code of Practice on Disinformation), and hosts various other reports. *Relevance to IBD:* Timely insights can alert stakeholders to new or evolving IBD campaigns. Policy analyses cover crucial regulatory developments impacting the digital platforms where IBD often spreads, contributing to discussions on platform accountability.

Spotlight on Specific Reports, Toolkits & Guides

Beyond the major hubs like EUvsDisinfo and EDMO, numerous organizations produce specific, high-value resources directly relevant to understanding and countering IBD. These resources range from analytical reports identifying trends and tactics to practical guides offering concrete strategies for intervention and resilience.

- **From Organizations Listed Above:**
  - **ISD:** Offers a rich library of reports directly tackling IBD. Examples include "Votes and Vitriol" and "Crushing Comments," which analyze gendered online abuse targeting women candidates in French and EU elections; "Hidden hate," exploring the use of Amharic to evade hate speech detection on TikTok; "Conflict Amplified,"

examining disinformation and hate related to the Israel-Hamas war; and "A resurgent and diversifying threat," analyzing Islamist extremist violence post-October 7. Their explainers, like the one on the antisemitic "Goyim Defense League (GDL)", provide concise overviews of specific hate groups. These resources offer deep dives into how gender, ethnicity, religion, and extremist ideologies intersect in the online space.

- **CCDH:** Known for impactful reports often focused on platform accountability and specific harms. Examples include investigations identifying key spreaders of disinformation (often involving identity-related hate), reports on platform failures to enforce policies against hate speech (e.g., "Failure to Protect," analysis of Meta's policy changes), and research exposing algorithmic harms like YouTube pushing eating disorder content to young girls. Practical resources include their "Parents Guide" for online safety and their "Digital & Information Resilience Training" for individuals and organizations. Their STAR Framework outlines principles for platform reform (Safety, Transparency, Accountability, Responsibility).

- **HOPE not hate:** Their flagship annual "State of Hate" report provides a comprehensive overview of the far-right landscape and hate trends in the UK. They also publish other in-depth investigations into specific extremist groups and narratives prevalent in the UK. Users seeking analysis of UK-specific anti-immigrant, anti-Muslim, or anti-LGBTQ+ narratives from the far-right should consult their publications list directly.

- **CST:** Produces the authoritative annual "Antisemitic Incidents Report" for the UK, alongside other publications offering detailed statistics and analysis of antisemitic trends, threats, and discourse. Their resources provide deep expertise specifically on antisemitism.

- **Glitch:** Focuses on the intersection of race, gender, and online safety. They offer resources tailored to the experiences of Black women and other marginalized groups facing online abuse, algorithmic bias, and tech injustice.

- **PERIL:** Develops evidence-based resources using a public health framework. These include toolkits, guides, media literacy interventions, videos, and training programs designed to prevent identity-based radicalization and build community resilience. Users should check PERIL's website for specific resource titles aimed at educators, community leaders, and individuals.

- **UNESCO:** Offers crucial educational and policy resources. Key guides include "Addressing hate speech through education: a guide for policy-makers", a guide for journalists on covering hate speech, and guidance for teachers on addressing conspiracy theories. Important reports cover "Technology-facilitated gender-based violence...", "History under attack: Holocaust denial...", and "Addressing hate speech on social media: contemporary challenges". These focus on building long-term resilience through education and media literacy, addressing specific identity targets like gender and religious/ethnic minorities.

– **UN OSAPG:** Central resources include the UN Strategy and Plan of Action on Hate Speech itself, along with various Guidance Notes applying the strategy to specific contexts (e.g., COVID-19 related hate speech, engaging media, engaging religious leaders). They offer a training course on the UN Strategy and have developed a "Comprehensive Methodology for Monitoring Social Media to Address and Counter Online Hate Speech". These resources are vital for understanding the UN's framework and approach to preventing incitement and related atrocity crimes.

– **Council of Europe (CoE):** Provides foundational policy documents like Recommendation CM/Rec(2022)16 on Combating Hate Speech and ECRI's General Policy Recommendation No. 15. Its Knowledge Hub curates valuable resources from CSOs and others, such as Tell MAMA's report on anti-Muslim hate in the UK, ILGA Europe's guide for effective LGBTI campaign narratives, and the Safe Journalists Network campaign materials on hate targeting women journalists. The Parliamentary Assembly also offers a "Toolkit on hate speech" for parliamentarians.

- **EU DisinfoLab:** A key resource is the "OSINT Toolkit to Detect and Analyse IBD-focused FIMI," developed with EEAS. They also publish reports on specific disinformation campaigns (e.g., Doppelganger), analyses of platform policies regarding misinformation, and research on identifying Coordinated Inauthentic Behaviour (CIB). Their focus is often on the technical and investigative aspects of uncovering IBD.

- **ADL:** Core resources include the interactive H.E.A.T. Map for tracking incidents, the extensive Hate Symbols Database, and the Glossary of Extremism. Their annual Audit of Antisemitic Incidents is a benchmark report, supplemented by reports on specific trends like white supremacist propaganda and bias in AI. These are essential for monitoring hate manifestations.

- **SPLC:** Provides the Hate Map for visualizing group locations, the Extremist Files database profiling groups/individuals, the annual "Year in Hate & Extremism" report analyzing trends, and numerous investigative articles on Hatewatch exposing specific extremist activities and identity-based hate rhetoric. These resources focus on tracking and exposing organized hate groups, primarily on the American right.

- **OSCE (Office of the Representative on Freedom of the Media - RFoM):** Publishes the comprehensive Safety of Journalists Guidebook (now in its 3rd edition), which addresses threats and state obligations. They issue Special Reports on topics like data collection on attacks against journalists, legal harassment (SLAPPs) against media, and the handling of media during public assemblies. The RFoM website curates resources by theme, including Hate Speech and Safety of Journalists. The office also issues Joint Declarations with other international rapporteurs on emerging threats.

- **Academic/University Reports:** Several recent academic publications offer valuable conceptual and empirical insights. Examples include Bradshaw's paper for the Stanley Center on "Disinformation and Identity-Based Violence", research published by the Royal Society on identity-based interventions to counter misinformation, the Hybrid CoE's strategic analysis "Identity as a tool for disinformation", and Gehrke et al.'s paper on "Disinformation and Identity-based Features…". These resources delve into the theoretical underpinnings, psychological mechanisms, and potential intervention strategies related to IBD.

- **Digital Rights Groups (Article 19):** Offers reports like "The Digital Silk Road: China and the Rise of Digital Oppression in the Indo-Pacific," analyzing state-sponsored digital repression impacting rights. Their Handbook on Content Moderation, developed for a UNESCO project, provides analysis grounded in freedom of expression standards. They also contribute analysis through participation in events discussing information integrity, wartime speech limitations, and surveillance targeting marginalized groups.

- – **Other Guides:** Resources like the Canadian Government's "Countering Disinformation: A Guidebook for Public Servants" offer general frameworks and tactics (e.g., pre-bunking, debunking) that are applicable to countering IBD, even if not specifically focused on identity.

This compilation reveals a crucial distinction within the resource landscape. Some resources excel at **monitoring and analysis**, providing data and insights into the scope and nature of the IBD problem (e.g., databases like EUvsDisinfo's or ADL's H.E.A.T. Map; analytical reports like SPLC's "Year in Hate" or CST's incident reports). Others focus primarily on **intervention and resilience-building**, offering practical strategies, educational approaches, and tools for counteraction (e.g., UNESCO's educational guides, EU DisinfoLab's OSINT toolkit, CCDH's resilience training, PERIL's prevention tools, ILGA Europe's counter-narrative guide). Users of this guide will benefit from a review both types of resources—those that help understand the threat and those that provide additional potentially complementary approaches to the Positive Identity Expansion approach detailed here.

A significant trend emerging from these resources is the increasing centrality of **Open Source Intelligence (OSINT)** techniques for investigating and exposing identity-based disinformation, particularly when it forms part of coordinated FIMI campaigns. The dedicated OSINT guidelines and toolkits developed by EUvsDisinfo/EEAS and EU DisinfoLab specifically for IBD/FIMI underscore this shift. These resources emphasize methodologies for systematically archiving digital evidence, assessing coordination between malicious actors, verifying the authenticity of content and perpetrators, tracing the origins of attacks, and evaluating the impact of disinformation operations using publicly available information. This signals a move towards more technical, investigative approaches necessary to unravel the often complex and covert nature of sophisticated IBD campaigns, complementing traditional content analysis. We feel this OSINT approach is very compatible with the intention of this guide to be applicable for the general practitioner with all nessesary steps to the method being introduced within an open source document. This guide's approach thus aims to broaded the OSINT practitioner's ability to go beyond evidence gathering, archiving and exposure of IBD network and techniques, to actually affecting change on the impact of IBD through increasing the identity resilience to the IBD among target populations.

Conclusion: Towards a More Resilient Response

Crucially, the resources listed above have been selected and described with a specific focus on their relevance to understanding and combating the **weaponization of identity**. This includes databases that track identity-targeting narratives, reports analyzing the tactics used against specific groups (based on gender, race, religion, sexual orientation, etc.), toolkits providing investigative methods for IBD, and educational materials designed to build resilience against identity-based manipulation.

The inclusion of resources ranging from high-level policy guidance (UN, CoE) and large-scale monitoring databases (EUvsDisinfo, ADL, SPLC) to practical intervention tools (ISD, CCDH, PERIL, EU DisinfoLab OSINT toolkit) and community-focused initiatives (Glitch, Strong Cities Network, ALA) provides this guide's readers with a multi-layered set of options. Readers wishing to expand their counter IBD work beyond that described within this toolkit can use these resources to:

- **Understand the Threat:** Access data and analysis on how IBD manifests, who perpetrates it, and which identities are targeted.

- **Identify Tactics:** Recognize the specific narratives, rhetorical devices, and manipulative techniques used in IBD campaigns beyond examples given in this guide.

- **Find Evidence-Based Information:** Consult credible sources for fact-checks, research findings, and expert analysis.

- **Access Practical Guidance:** Utilize other toolkits, training materials, and best practices for developing countermeasures and building individual or community resilience.

Navigating the complex challenge of identity-based disinformation requires both deep understanding and practical strategies. By drawing on the diverse expertise and resources outlined here, users can contribute more broadly to fostering information environments that are more resilient to manipulation and more respectful of human dignity and diversity. It is recommended that users explore these organizations and resources further, selecting those most relevant to their specific needs, contexts, and objectives in the ongoing effort to counter identity-based disinformation.

14 Guidance on Using AI Tools Responsibly

Artificial Intelligence (AI) tools, such as large language models (LLMs) like ChatGPT, Claude, Gemini, and others, can be powerful aids in analyzing information and drafting narratives as outlined in this toolkit. The prompt library provides examples to help leverage these tools. However, using AI requires awareness and responsibility.

Key Considerations:

1. **AI is a Tool, Not a Replacement for Judgment:** AI can generate text, summarize information, and brainstorm ideas, but it lacks true understanding, cultural nuance, and ethical reasoning. **Always** critically review, edit, and adapt AI-generated output. Your knowledge of the specific context and audience is irreplaceable.

2. **Potential for Bias:** AI models are trained on vast datasets from the internet, which contain existing societal biases (racial, gender, cultural, political, etc.). Models may inadvertently reproduce or even amplify these biases.

   - **Be Aware:** Different models (e.g., those from OpenAI, Anthropic, Google, Meta, xAI) may have different inherent biases based on their training data and fine-tuning. There is no single "unbiased" model.

- **Critically Evaluate:** Question AI outputs that seem stereotypical, one-sided, or lack diverse perspectives. Explicitly ask the AI to consider alternative viewpoints or check for bias in its own response.

3. **Accuracy and "Hallucinations":** LLMs can sometimes generate plausible-sounding but incorrect information, often called "hallucinations." They may invent facts, sources, or details.

    - **Fact-Check:** Independently verify any factual claims, statistics, or historical references generated by AI before using them. Do not assume AI output is accurate.

4. **Privacy and Data Security:** Be mindful of the data you input into AI tools, especially public-facing ones.

    - **Avoid Sensitive Information:** Do not input personally identifiable information (PII), confidential community details, or sensitive strategic plans into public AI models unless you understand and accept the platform's data usage policies. Consider using models with stronger privacy guarantees or enterprise versions if handling sensitive data.

5. **Ethical Oversight:** AI cannot determine if a narrative strategy is ethically sound.

    - **Apply Ethical Frameworks:** Use the ethical guidelines and checklists provided in this toolkit (Chapter 7 and Chapter 15) to evaluate any AI-assisted narrative development. The responsibility for ethical use remains entirely with you.

6. **Authenticity:** AI-generated text can sometimes sound generic or lack the authentic voice of a community.

- **Adapt and Personalize:** Heavily edit AI drafts to match the specific language, tone, and cultural style of your target audience and chosen communication channel. Infuse it with genuine human experience and insight.

Tips for Effective Prompting:

- **Be Specific:** Clearly define the task, target audience, desired tone, and key constraints.
- **Provide Context:** Give the AI relevant background information about the IBD, the audience's values, and your strategic goals (while respecting privacy).
- **Iterate:** Don't expect perfect results on the first try. Refine your prompts based on the AI's output. Ask follow-up questions.
- **Assign a Role:** Sometimes telling the AI to act as a specific persona (e.g., "Act as a community historian," "Act as a communications strategist sensitive to cultural nuances") can yield better results.
- **Request Multiple Options:** Ask for several different narrative ideas or message drafts to give you more to work with.
- **Explicitly Ask for Checks:** Include requests like "check for potential bias," "consider alternative perspectives," or "ensure the tone is positive and inclusive" in your prompts.

Scaling with AI for Organizations

While the prompts provided in this toolkit are designed for individual use and learning, the underlying principles can be significantly scaled up. Organizations undertaking larger campaigns can leverage AI tools, potentially including more advanced prompts or workflows available through OICD, to automate and accelerate key parts of the process, such as:

- **Large-scale IBD Analysis:** Processing and categorizing large volumes of potentially harmful content.
- **Audience Segmentation:** Identifying nuanced subgroups within a target audience based on online discourse.
- **Narrative Generation at Scale:** Creating diverse sets of alternative narrative messages tailored to different segments and platforms.
- **Impact Monitoring:** Analyzing audience responses and engagement patterns across multiple channels.

Using AI for scaling requires careful planning, robust ethical oversight, and often more sophisticated technical setups, but it offers a powerful way to translate the toolkit's methods into broad, actionable campaigns.

By using AI tools thoughtfully and responsibly, you can enhance your ability to analyze information and develop effective alternative narratives, while always maintaining critical human oversight and ethical judgment.

15 AI Prompts for IBD Analysis

Note: AI is a tool to assist your thinking, not replace it. Please review the **Guidance on Using AI Tools Responsibly** chapter before utilizing these prompts. Always apply ethical judgment and critically evaluate AI outputs, ensuring they align with the toolkit's principles and your understanding of the specific context.

Paste the following into an AI model with a capacity equal to or larger than Claude 3.5 / Gemini 2.0

```
1   I'm analyzing an identity-based disinformation (IBD)
        campaign targeting [describe target audience]. I've
        collected these examples of the disinformation:
2
3   [Share 3-5 examples of IBD messages with direct quotes if
        possible]
4
5   Could you help me:
6
7   1.  Identify the main themes and narratives in these
        messages with respect to how they restrict the target
        audience's identity (potentially through their use of a
        representation of other)
8   2.  Analyze which emotions they're trying to evoke (fear,
        pride, resentment, etc.)
9   3.  Determine which fundamental needs they're exploiting (
        belonging, security, self-esteem, etc.)
10  4.  Identify how they're manipulating identity (what narrow
        version of identity they're promoting)
11  5.  Spot any false choices or "us vs them" framing
12
13  Please avoid amplifying the harmful content. Focus on
        analyzing the tactics so I can develop positive
        alternatives.
```

16 AI Prompts for Audience Analysis

Note: AI is a tool to assist your thinking, not replace it. Please review the **Guidance on Using AI Tools Responsibly** chapter before utilizing these prompts. Always apply ethical judgment and critically evaluate AI outputs, ensuring they align with the toolkit's principles and your understanding of the specific context.

Paste the following into an AI model with a capacity equal to or larger than Claude 3.5 / Gemini 2.0

```
1   I'm working to counter identity-based disinformation in my
        community. I need help understanding my target audience
        (the people being influenced by the disinformation,
        not those being attacked). Here's what I know about
        them so far:
2
3   [Describe demographics, values, concerns, and cultural
        context of your audience]
4
5   Can you help me create a comprehensive profile of this
        audience, including:
6
7   1.  Core demographics and identity layers
8   2.  Their fundamental psychological needs (belonging,
        security, esteem, etc.)
9   3.  Values that matter most to them
10  4.  Potential pain points or vulnerabilities
11  5.  How they typically receive information
12
```

Please focus on building a nuanced, respectful
understanding that acknowledges diversity within **this**
group.

17 AI Prompts for Narrative Creation

Note: AI is a tool to assist your thinking, not replace it. Please review the **Guidance on Using AI Tools Responsibly** chapter before utilizing these prompts. Always apply ethical judgment and critically evaluate AI outputs, ensuring they align with the toolkit's principles and your understanding of the specific context.

Ensure that you insert your info inside the [ ] within the prompt
You may also wish to paste the contents of step 3 from the implementation guide at the end of the prompt.

```
1  I'm developing 'equal alternative narratives' to counter
       identity-based disinformation targeting [describe
       target audience, including key values, needs, and
       cultural context from Step 2 analysis].
2
3  My analysis from Step 1 shows the IBD is:
4  *   Exploiting these core needs: [list needs like belonging
       , security, esteem, justice]
5  *   Using these manipulation tactics/emotions: [summarize
       key IBD tactics, e.g., fear-mongering, promoting
       exclusion, distorting values]
6  *   Promoting this narrow identity framing: [describe the
       restrictive identity pushed by IBD]
7
8  Based on this understanding of the IBD (Step 1) and my
       target audience (Step 2), could you help me brainstorm
       for Step 3:
9
```

1. **Infer Positive Values to Emphasize (Part 3A):** Based on the IBD tactics and the audience's known values, what positive values are being undermined, distorted, or are the opposite of the IBD's framing? (e.g., community, inclusion, fairness, resilience, critical thinking, authentic tradition).

2. **Generate Alternative Ways to Fulfill Needs (Part 3A):** For each need exploited by the IBD [list the needs again], suggest concrete, healthy, and culturally resonant ways this audience could fulfill that need, drawing on their existing community resources, aspirations, or cultural elements. Aim for multiple options per need.

3. **Develop Narrative Strategies (Part 3B):** Based on the inferred values and alternative fulfillments, suggest 3-5 specific narrative angles or strategies that focus on identity expansion, avoid mentioning the 'Other', circumvent backlash, and meet needs authentically. (e.g., "Strategy: Celebrate internal community diversity to broaden 'us' and fulfill belonging need").

4. **Find Cultural References (Part 3C):** Suggest relevant cultural references (figures, stories, proverbs, events, practices) from [mention audience's culture/region **if** known] that could authentically support these narrative strategies and resonate deeply with the audience.

Remember: The goal is NOT to directly counter the IBD, but to **expand identity options** positively. Please avoid mentioning any "other" group the IBD targets and focus on constructive, inclusive alternatives rooted in the target audience's context.

I'm creating social media content (Step 5) based on my narrative development (Step 3) for [describe audience]. My chosen narrative framework focuses on:

* Values to emphasize: [list values derived from the prompt above]
* Needs to address & Alternative Fulfillments: [list needs and the positive ways to meet them derived from the prompt above]
* Narrative Strategies/Angles: [list strategies derived from the prompt above]
* Key Cultural References: [list references derived from the prompt above]

```
 7
 8  Can you help me draft 5-7 social media posts that:
 9
10  1.  Expand identity options rather than narrowing them
11  2.  Fulfill the psychological needs being exploited by IBD,
        but in healthy ways
12  3.  Use authentic language that would resonate with this
        audience
13  4.  Incorporate relevant cultural references in a natural
        way
14  5.  Include appropriate hashtags and engagement prompts
15
16  For each post, please specify:
17
18  *   The platform it's designed for (Facebook, Instagram,
        Twitter, etc.)
19  *   The type of content (text, image description, video
        concept)
20  *   The specific need/value it addresses
21  *   How it expands identity options
22
23  Remember: Do NOT mention or directly counter the IBD. Focus
        ONLY on positive expansion.
```

18 AI Prompts for Ethical Review

Note: AI is a tool to assist your thinking, not replace it. Please review the **Guidance on Using AI Tools Responsibly** chapter before utilizing these prompts. Always apply ethical judgment and critically evaluate AI outputs, ensuring they align with the toolkit's principles and your understanding of the specific context. AI *cannot* make ethical judgments for you.

```
1  I've refined my messages countering identity-based
       disinformation and now need to conduct a final ethical
       review before sharing. My target audience is [describe
       audience] and here are my messages:
2  [Insert your finalized messages]
3
4  Please help me:
5  1. Evaluate these messages against ethical guidelines (
       accuracy, respect for diversity, transparency, do no
       harm)
6  2. Identify any unintended consequences or risks
7  3. Suggest a strategic approach for sequencing and sharing
       these messages (timing, frequency, engagement strategy)
8  4. Recommend ways to monitor impact and adapt based on
       audience response
9  5. Develop a self-care plan for managing this work, which
       can be emotionally demanding
10
11 Please be thorough in your ethical assessment - I want to
       ensure these messages build bridges rather than walls.
```

19 AI Prompts for Identifying Trusted Voices and Channels

Note: AI is a tool to assist your thinking, not replace it. Please review the **Guidance on Using AI Tools Responsibly** chapter before utilizing these prompts. Always apply ethical judgment and critically evaluate AI outputs, ensuring they align with the toolkit's principles and your understanding of the specific context.

```
1  I'm working to counter identity-based disinformation
       affecting [describe audience]. To effectively reach
       this audience (as per Step 4 of the implementation
       guide), I need to identify trusted voices and
       communication channels.
2
3  Based on what I know about this audience [share relevant
       details from Step 2 analysis], can you help me:
4
5  1.  Suggest categories of potential trusted voices within
       this community (e.g., types of community leaders,
       professions, roles, informal influencers).
6  2.  Brainstorm communication channels (both online and
       offline) that this audience likely uses and trusts.
7  3.  Provide a framework or criteria for evaluating the
       trustworthiness and potential influence of these voices
       and channels within this specific community context.
8  4.  Suggest specific questions I should research or ask (e.
       g., through informal conversations or observation) to
       better understand who and what this audience trusts?
9
10  Please focus on authentic, respected voices and channels *
       within* the community rather than relying solely on
       external authorities or generic platforms.
```

20 Implementation Timeline and Planning Worksheet

Use this worksheet to plan and track your implementation of the Reclaiming Our Narrative toolkit. Each step links to detailed guidance in the toolkit.

Step 1: Analyze the IBD Campaign

Detailed guidance in Step 2 of Implementation Steps

Use the IBD Analysis Template to complete this step.

Timeline: _____

Key Milestones: - [ ] Gather IBD examples - [ ] Identify themes and patterns - [ ] Analyze emotional manipulation tactics - [ ] Document false choices and identity narrowing

Step 2: Define and Understand Your Target Audience

Detailed guidance in Step 1 of Implementation Steps

Use the Audience Analysis Template to complete this step.

Timeline: _____

Key Milestones: - [ ] Complete initial audience research - [ ] Develop audience archetype - [ ] Document identity layers and needs - [ ] Review with community members

Step 3: Develop Equal Alternative Narratives

Detailed guidance in Step 3 of Implementation Steps

Use the Narrative Development Worksheet to complete this step.

Timeline: _____

Key Milestones: - [ ] Identify positive values to amplify - [ ] Develop narrative strategies - [ ] Find cultural references - [ ] Create message framework

Step 4: Identify Trusted Voices and Channels

Detailed guidance in Step 4 of Implementation Steps

Timeline: _____

Key Milestones: - [ ] Map trusted community voices - [ ] Assess communication channels - [ ] Validate with community members - [ ] Document outreach strategy

Step 5: Craft Your Equal Alternative Narratives

Detailed guidance in Step 5 of Implementation Steps

Timeline: _____

Key Milestones: - [ ] Draft initial messages - [ ] Add cultural enhance-ments - [ ] Adapt for platforms - [ ] Document message variations

Step 6: Strategic Narrative Design

Detailed guidance in Step 6 of Implementation Steps

Timeline: _____

Key Milestones: - [ ] Conduct invisibility assessment - [ ] Refine for subtlety - [ ] Plan contingency responses - [ ] Build support networks

Step 7: Review, Refine, and Share Responsibly

Detailed guidance in Step 7 of Implementation Steps

Use the Ethics Checklist for final review.

Timeline: _____

Key Milestones: - [ ] Complete ethics review - [ ] Gather community feedback - [ ] Refine based on input - [ ] Create monitoring plan

Overall Project Timeline

Project Start Date: _____ Target Completion Date: _____

Resources Needed

Personnel: - Project Lead: _____ - Community Liaisons: _____ - Content Creators: _____ - Cultural Advisors: _____

Tools/Materials: -   _____   -   _____   - _____

Budget: - _____

Notes and Adjustments

Use this space to document any changes to the plan, learnings, or important considerations:

_____

_____

_____

Review Schedule

Weekly Check-in Day/Time: _____ Monthly Review Day: _____ Quarterly Assessment Date: _____

Remember to regularly consult the ethical guidelines and best practices throughout implementation.

21 IBD Analysis Template

Reference: Step 1 of Implementation Steps

IBD Examples Collection

Document examples of identity-based disinformation you've encountered:

Social Media Posts

- Screenshot/Link: _____
- Content: _____
- Platform: _____
- Date observed: _____

Articles/Blog Posts

- URL: _____
- Key points: _____
- Publication/Site: _____
- Date: _____

Memes/Images

- Description: _____
- Context: _____
- Where found: _____
- Date observed: _____

Videos

- Link/Source: _____
- Key messages: _____
- Platform: _____
- Date: _____

Conversations/Discussions

- Context: _____
- Key points: _____
- Setting: _____
- Date: _____

Theme Analysis

Main Narratives

List recurring themes and patterns in the IBD messages:

1. Theme: _____ Examples: _____ Frequency: _____

2. Theme: _____ Examples: _____ Frequency: _____

3. Theme: _____ Examples: _____ Frequency: _____

Emotional Analysis

Positive Emotions Used

Note how these are often used deceptively:

- ☐ Pride Context: _____
- ☐ Belonging Context: _____
- ☐ Hope Context: _____

Negative Emotions Triggered

- ☐ Fear Context: _____
- ☐ Anger Context: _____
- ☐ Resentment Context: _____
- ☐ Insecurity Context: _____
- ☐ Distrust Context: _____

Needs Analysis

Focus on how the message fulfills the receiver's needs from their perspective.

Belonging and Love

From the receiver's perspective, how does this IBD message fulfill their need for Belonging and Love?

Promises made: _____ Tactics used: _____
Emotional triggers: _____

Self-Esteem, Status & Significance

From the receiver's perspective, how does this IBD message fulfill their need for Self-Esteem, Status & Significance?

Promises made: _____ Tactics used: _____
Emotional triggers: _____

Equality & Justice

From the receiver's perspective, how does this IBD message fulfill their need for Equality & Justice (even if distorted)?

Promises made: _____ Tactics used: _____
Emotional triggers: _____

Freedom from Fear and Suffering (Security)

From the receiver's perspective, how does this IBD message fulfill their need for Security?

Promises made: _____ Tactics used: _____
Emotional triggers: _____

Identity Manipulation Analysis

Narrow Identity Promotion

What restricted version of identity is being pushed?

Description: _____ Key elements: _____ Impact: _____

Suppressed Identity Aspects

What aspects of identity are being discredited or minimized?

1. _____

2. _____

3. _____

False Choices Analysis

Document "either/or" statements that force false choices:

1. Choice presented: _____ Reality: _____

2. Choice presented: _____ Reality: _____

3. Choice presented: _____ Reality: _____

Summary Analysis

Main Themes

Summarize the key narratives: _____ _____

Emotional Tactics

List primary emotional manipulation strategies: _____
_____

Need Exploitation

Document how fundamental needs are being targeted: _____
_____

Identity Manipulation

Describe the key identity manipulation tactics: _____
_____

False Choices

List the main false choices being presented: _____
_____

Supporting Examples

Include specific examples that illustrate each element:

1. Example: _____ Illustrates: _____

2. Example: _____ Illustrates: _____

3. Example: _____ Illustrates: _____

Next Steps

- ☐ Share analysis with project team
- ☐ Update Narrative Development Worksheet with insights
- ☐ Identify gaps requiring additional monitoring
- ☐ Document emerging patterns or changes in IBD tactics

Need help with this analysis? See the AI prompts for IBD analysis

.

22 Audience Analysis Template

Reference: Step 2 of Implementation Steps

Core Demographics

Age Composition

What age ranges are most affected? Consider different generational experiences and values.

Notes: _____ _____

Geographic Context

Where do they live? Consider urban/rural differences, regional cultural variations, and local history.

Notes: _____ _____

Cultural Background

What are their cultural, ethnic, religious, and linguistic backgrounds? Look for diversity within these categories.

Notes: _____ _____

Socioeconomic Factors

Consider income levels, types of employment, education levels, and economic concerns.

Notes: _____ _____

Identity Ecosystem

Identity Layers

What are the multiple identities held by this audience? (e.g., professional, religious, cultural, familial, regional)

Notes: _____ _____

Identity Hierarchy

Which identity aspects are most salient or valued in different contexts?

Notes: _____ _____

Identity Tensions

Where do they experience pressure or conflict between different aspects of identity?

Notes: _____ _____

Identity Evolution

How have their collective identities changed over time? What aspects have remained constant?

Notes: _____ _____

Core Cultural Narratives & Beliefs

What core cultural stories, myths, historical narratives, or foundational beliefs are central to this audience's identity and worldview? How do prevalent religious or traditional beliefs influence their views on relevant topics?

Notes: _____ _____

Psychological Profile

Core Values

What principles guide their decisions and worldview? (e.g., family, tradition, freedom, security, progress)

Notes: _____ _____

Fundamental Needs

Which psychological needs are most important to them? (belonging, self-esteem, security, meaning)

Notes: _____ _____

Pain Points

What concerns, anxieties, or threats do they perceive to their identity and way of life?

Notes: _____ _____

Aspirations

What are their hopes for themselves, their families, and their communities?

Notes: _____ _____

Cultural Influences on Values/Needs

How do specific cultural contexts (traditions, history, religion) shape the expression or prioritization of their core values and fundamental needs?

Notes: _____ _____

Information Landscape

Trust Networks

Who do they consider credible and trustworthy sources of information?

Notes: _____ _____

Digital Presence

Which platforms, online communities, and media channels do they engage with regularly?

Notes: _____ _____

Information Consumption

How do they typically receive and process information? (formats, timing, context)

Notes: _____ _____

Social Influencers

Which community leaders, public figures, or everyday individuals shape their perspectives?

Notes: _____ _____

Research Methods Used

Direct Engagement

- ☐ Informal conversations
- ☐ Community events attendance
- ☐ Active listening sessions

Notes: _____ _____

Digital Ethnography

- ☐ Platform observation
- ☐ Content analysis
- ☐ Language pattern analysis

Notes: _____ _____

Historical Context

- ☐ Community history research
- ☐ Cultural traditions study
- ☐ Media representation review

Notes: _____ _____

Audience Archetype Development

Primary Archetype Description

Create a rich, nuanced portrait of your target audience. Include demographics, values, and key characteristics.

_____

_____

_____

_____

Audience Variations

Note important variations within your target audience:

1. _____
2. _____
3. _____
4. _____

Vulnerability Assessment

Identify specific vulnerabilities that IBD might exploit:

1. _____
2. _____
3. _____
4. _____

Documentation Summary

Key Identity Components

List the most important aspects of identity discovered:

1. _____
2. _____
3. _____
4. _____

Authentic Communication Channels

List the most effective ways to reach this audience:

1. _____

2. _____

3. _____

4. _____

Cultural References

Note specific language, references, and values that resonate:

1. _____

2. _____

3. _____

4. _____

Next Steps

☐ Review completed analysis with community members
☐ Update IBD Analysis Template with relevant insights
☐ Share key findings with project team
☐ Document any gaps requiring additional research

Remember: The more deeply you understand your audience, the more effectively you can create narratives that expand their identity options rather than narrowing them.

Need help with this analysis? See the AI prompts for audience analysis

23 Narrative Development Worksheet

Reference: Step 3 of Implementation Steps

This worksheet helps you translate your analysis from Steps 1 & 2 into actionable narrative strategies, following the structure of Step 3 in the main guide.

Part 3A: Identify Positive Values & Alternative Need Fulfillment

Use your analysis from the IBD Analysis Worksheet and the Audience Analysis Worksheet to answer the following for each key need exploited by the IBD:

Underlying Need: (e.g., Belonging and Love) _____

1. **How IBD Exploits This Need:** (Summarize from Step 1 & 2 analysis)

   - _____
   - _____

2. **Infer Positive Values to Emphasize:** (Use guiding questions from main guide's Step 3A.1: What's the opposite? What's

undermined? What's distorted? What does audience value? What universal values apply?)

- Value 1: _____ (Rationale: _____)
- Value 2: _____ (Rationale: _____)
- Value 3: _____ (Rationale: _____)

3. **Generate Alternative Ways to Fulfill This Need:** (Use guiding questions from main guide's Step 3A.2: What already exists? How can aspirations be channeled? What cultural resources? How to offer multiple options?)

- Alternative 1: _____ (Rationale/Connection to Audience: _____)
- Alternative 2: _____ (Rationale/Connection to Audience: _____)
- Alternative 3: _____ (Rationale/Connection to Audience: _____)

(Repeat for each relevant Underlying Need: Self-Esteem/Status/Significanc Equality/Justice, Security)

Part 3B: Develop Equal Alternative Narrative Strategies

Based on the values and alternative fulfillments identified above, brainstorm specific narrative strategies. Remember the core principles: Expand identity options, avoid mentioning the "Other," circumvent backlash, meet needs authentically.

Narrative Strategy 1: * Focus (Value/Need): _____ * Angle/Approach: (How will you frame this? e.g., Celebrate internal diversity, highlight local resilience, showcase multiple paths to success) _____ * Key Message Idea: _____ * How it Expands Identity: _____ * How it Avoids Backlash: _____

Narrative Strategy 2: * Focus (Value/Need): _____ * Angle/Approach: _____ * Key Message Idea: _____ * How it Expands Identity: _____ * How it Avoids Backlash: _____

(Add more strategies as needed)

Part 3C: Find Cultural References

Use this section to brainstorm specific cultural elements (drawing from Step 2 analysis and the prompts below) that can bring your narrative strategies to life. Go beyond obvious symbols. Explore deeper cultural elements that resonate with the audience's core identity and worldview. Consider:

- **Foundational Stories/Myths:** What are the origin stories, creation myths, or foundational narratives widely known and respected within this culture?
- **Core Traditions/Rituals:** What are the central traditions, rituals, or ceremonies that express core values or mark important life events? How are they practiced locally?
- **Influential Art/Music/Literature:** What specific works of art, music, or literature hold significant cultural meaning or reflect shared experiences?
- **Local Interpretations:** How are broader cultural or religious tenets interpreted and practiced specifically within this local

community?

- **Resilience Narratives:** What stories exist within the culture about overcoming past hardships or adapting to change while maintaining identity?

Famous Figures

People who embody multiple, seemingly contradictory values:

1. Name: _____ Values demonstrated: _____
   Relevant story: _____

2. Name: _____ Values demonstrated: _____
   Relevant story: _____

Literary Works

Books, poems, or stories that celebrate complexity:

1. Title: _____ Key themes: _____ Relevant excerpt: _____

2. Title: _____ Key themes: _____ Relevant excerpt: _____

Proverbs/Idioms

Sayings that reflect adaptability and inclusive values:

1. Saying: _____   Meaning: _____
   Context: _____

2. Saying: _____ Meaning: _____
    Context: _____

Historical Events

Events demonstrating cooperation and mutual support:

1. Event: _____ Key lesson: _____ Modern relevance: _____

2. Event: _____ Key lesson: _____ Modern relevance: _____

Deeper Cultural Elements (Brainstorming)

Use the prompts above to brainstorm less obvious but potentially more powerful cultural references:

1. Element: _____ (e.g., Specific local legend, interpretation of a religious text, community adaptation story) Relevance/Meaning: _____ Potential Use: _____

2. Element: _____ Relevance/Meaning: _____ Potential Use: _____

Trusted Voices and Channels

Reference: Step 4 of Implementation Steps

Community Leaders

- Name: _____ Role: _____ Influence area: _____ Potential involvement: _____

Communication Channels

- Channel: _____ Reach: _____ Best content type: _____ Engagement strategy: _____

Message Development

Reference: Step 5 of Implementation Steps

This section guides you through crafting specific messages based on your narrative framework (from Part 3D) and chosen voices/channels (from Step 4).

1. Draft Basic Message Framework (Using Step 3D Framework)

For each key narrative strategy/angle identified in your framework: * Core message idea: _____ * Supporting points/story elements: _____ * Potential visual ideas: _____ * Desired emotional resonance: _____

2. Cultural Enhancement (Using Step 3C References)

How will you weave in the cultural references identified earlier? *
Reference 1: _____ How to integrate: _____
* Reference 2: _____ How to integrate: _____

3. Platform Adaptation & Content Strategy (Using Step 4 Channels)

Voice and Tone Notes

- Authentic community language patterns: _____
- Key cultural touchpoints to include: _____
- Desired emotional tone: _____
- Language to avoid (e.g., activism markers): _____

Platform-Specific Content Plan

Platform: (e.g., Facebook Group) _____ * Content Format: (e.g., Story post with image) _____ * Draft Content/Caption: [Draft message tailored for this platform] * Visual Element Description: _____ * Hashtags/Engagement Prompt: _____ * Alignment with Step 3 Framework (Need/Value/Strategy): _____

Platform: (e.g., Twitter/X) _____ * Content Format: (e.g., Thread) _____ * Draft Content/Caption: [Draft message tailored for this platform] * Visual Element Description: _____ * Hashtags/Engagement Prompt: _____ * Alignment with Step 3 Framework (Need/Value/Strategy): _____

(Add more platforms as needed)

Message Documentation & Examples

(Use this section or a separate log to track final messages)

Message ID: [e.g., FB_Belonging_1] _____ * Need Addressed: _____ * Values Emphasized: _____ * Identity Expansion Strategy: _____ * Target Platform: _____ * Content Type: _____ * Final Caption/Text: `[Final message text]` * Visual Elements: _____ * Hashtags: _____ * Cultural References Used: _____ * Risk Assessment Notes: _____

Next Steps

- ☐ Review narratives with community members
- ☐ Test messages with small focus group
- ☐ Refine based on feedback
- ☐ Develop content calendar
- ☐ Create monitoring plan

Need help developing narratives? See: - AI prompts for narrative creation - Step 3: Develop Equal Alternative Narratives - Step 5: Craft Your Equal Alternative Narratives

24 Ethics Checklist

Reference: Step 7 of Implementation Steps

Content Quality Review

Accuracy Check

- ☐ All information is factually correct and verifiable
- ☐ Sources are reliable and can be cited if needed
- ☐ No exaggerations or unsubstantiated claims
- ☐ Cultural references are accurate and appropriate

Notes: _____

Authenticity Assessment

- ☐ Content genuinely resonates with target audience values
- ☐ Reflects real lived experiences of the community
- ☐ Uses authentic language and cultural references
- ☐ Avoids artificial or forced narratives

Notes: _____

Cultural Relevance

☐ Cultural references are meaningful to the audience
☐ Respects cultural nuances and sensitivities
☐ Incorporates community-specific context
☐ Avoids cultural appropriation

Notes: _____

Narrative Depth

☐ Content has sufficient complexity and nuance
☐ Avoids oversimplification of issues
☐ Maintains engagement while being accessible
☐ Reflects real-world complexity

Notes: _____

Strategic Effectiveness

Need Fulfillment

☐ Addresses same needs as IBD in healthy ways
☐ Provides constructive alternatives
☐ Maintains emotional authenticity
☐ Avoids manipulation tactics
☐ Ensures strategy genuinely empowers audience, not subtly manipulates

Notes: _____

Strategic Subtlety

- ☐ Appears as authentic cultural expression
- ☐ Avoids obvious counter-narrative markers
- ☐ Integrates naturally with existing narratives
- ☐ Maintains appropriate distance from IBD topics

Notes: _____

Identity Expansion

- ☐ Actively expands identity options
- ☐ Avoids creating new restrictions
- ☐ Celebrates diversity within community
- ☐ Provides multiple paths for expression

Notes: _____

Risk Assessment

Content Safety

- ☐ No references to targeted groups
- ☐ Avoids inflammatory language
- ☐ Considers potential misuse
- ☐ Protects vulnerable individuals
- ☐ Avoids validating factual claims or harmful premises of the IBD

Notes: _____

Misinterpretation Potential

- ☐ Clear and unambiguous messaging
- ☐ Limited potential for misunderstanding
- ☐ Considered alternative interpretations
- ☐ Included necessary context

Notes: _____

Unintended Implications

- ☐ Checked for problematic subtext
- ☐ Assessed potential negative impacts
- ☐ Considered various audience perspectives
- ☐ Evaluated long-term implications

Notes: _____

Cultural Sensitivities

- ☐ Respects cultural boundaries
- ☐ Avoids appropriation
- ☐ Considers historical context
- ☐ Maintains cultural integrity
- ☐ Ensures cultural authenticity doesn't justify harm or violate universal ethics

Notes: _____

Structural Elements

Clarity

☐ Message is clear and concise
☐ Language is accessible
☐ Key points are easily understood
☐ Complex concepts well-explained

Notes: _____

Language Appropriateness

☐ Matches community communication style
☐ Uses appropriate terminology
☐ Avoids jargon unless necessary
☐ Maintains consistent tone

Notes: _____

Emotional Balance

☐ Connects emotionally without manipulation
☐ Maintains appropriate tone
☐ Avoids trauma triggers
☐ Provides emotional support

Notes: _____

Implementation Ethics

Distribution Strategy

- ☐ Respects community channels
- ☐ Uses appropriate timing
- ☐ Considers local context
- ☐ Follows platform guidelines

Notes: _____

Community Involvement

- ☐ Includes community feedback
- ☐ Respects community leadership
- ☐ Maintains transparency
- ☐ Supports community ownership

Notes: _____

Impact Monitoring

- ☐ Has clear success metrics
- ☐ Includes feedback mechanisms
- ☐ Plans for adaptation
- ☐ Considers long-term effects

Notes: _____

Additional Considerations

Specific Concerns

List any specific ethical concerns for your context:

1. _____

2. _____

3. _____

Mitigation Strategies

Document how you'll address each concern:

1. _____

2. _____

3. _____

Final Review

Overall Assessment

☐ Meets all ethical guidelines
☐ Achieves strategic objectives
☐ Maintains community trust
☐ Ready for implementation

Required Changes

List any necessary modifications:

1. _____

2. _____

3. _____

Next Steps

- ☐ Incorporate feedback from review
- ☐ Document decisions and rationale
- ☐ Update related materials
- ☐ Schedule follow-up assessment

Remember to consult the ethical guidelines for additional guidance.

Need help with ethical review? See the AI prompts for ethical review

www.ingramcontent.com/pod-product-compliance
Lightning Source LLC
Chambersburg PA
CBHW052010030426
42334CB00029BA/3156